*EVANGELICALS, REVOLUTIONISTS
AND IDEALISTS*

Evangelicals, Revolutionists and Idealists

Six English Contributors to American Thought and Action

By

FRANCIS JOHN McCONNELL

A BISHOP OF THE METHODIST CHURCH

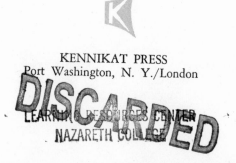

KENNIKAT PRESS
Port Washington, N. Y./London

EVANGELICALS, REVOLUTIONISTS AND IDEALISTS

Copyright 1942 by Whitmore and Stone
Reissued in 1972 by Kennikat Press by
arrangement with Abingdon Press
Library of Congress Catalog Card No: 75-153252
ISBN 0-8046-1505-5

Manufactured by Taylor Publishing Company   Dallas, Texas

ESSAY AND GENERAL LITERATURE INDEX REPRINT SERIES

To

ARLO AYRES BROWN

EDUCATOR

Wise in financial administration, in choice of teachers, in leadership of students, and in maintenance of standards

DREW LECTURESHIP IN BIOGRAPHY

THE Drew Lectureship in Biography was established in 1928 by President and Mrs. Ezra Squier Tipple, it being their desire to make accessible to the students of Drew Theological Seminary and the other students of Drew University an annual course of lectures in Christian Biography. Seven notable courses of lectures have already been given:

Voices of the New Room, T. Ferrier Hulme

Charles Wesley: Evangelist and Poet, F. Luke Wiseman

Creative Men: Our Fathers and Brethren, William Fraser McDowell

Men of Zeal, The Romance of American Methodist Beginnings, William Warren Sweet

Men of the Outposts, Herbert Welch

Saints in Action, Dumas Malone

Moral Leaders, Edward Howard Griggs

These lectures, the eighth in the series, were given in March, 1942.

PREFACE

It may not be easy to discover any large degree of unity in the relation of these chapters to one another. By the requirements of the lectureship the treatments are biographical. The chief aim of the author is to point out some influences of England on America in the eighteenth century which do not seem to have been sufficiently recognized. The England of the eighteenth century has not received the credit due for some phases of her attitude to America.

There is rather close relationship between the characters discussed here, though of varying degrees of intimacy and importance. The connections of Oglethorpe, Wesley, and Whitefield to one another are well enough known. Oglethorpe and Berkeley at least sought to work together in various plans to aid the colonies. Whitefield was a co-worker with Jonathan Edwards in the Great Awakening. One of Wesley's last letters was to Wilberforce concerning the slave trade. All of the above who were on the scene during the controversy over the deism of Thomas Paine were united in opposition to him. All including Paine could have fairly been called "utopians."

I use the word "evangelical" in the broader sense as indicating those deeply interested in the renewal of the religious life in the country, though not necessarily connected with the evangelical parties, so called.

FRANCIS JOHN McCONNELL

CONTENTS

JAMES EDWARD OGLETHORPE

IT may seem strange to begin a series on contributions of English Evangelicalism to America with a chapter on James Edward Oglethorpe. Oglethorpe was not an evangelical in the stricter meaning of the term; that is, he was not a member of any evangelical group in the Church of England in the eighteenth century; but he was a devout churchman, an associate of Wesley in the years immediately preceding the Great Revival, and he worked from a basis which might almost be called religious utopianism. True, the aims of the Georgia Company in England were mixed, looking quite as much to a buffer against Spain as to an example of colonial humanitarianism. It is true also that Oglethorpe's distinctive colonial contributions disappeared in the great social and political writings of the later movement after Oglethorpe had left America.

Oglethorpe, however, is worthy of lasting study for his attempts to lift imperialism into the realm of the higher human values. If imperialism is to survive today, it can be only by the recovery of the spirit and the aims of Oglethorpe. It is noteworthy that two excellent biographies of Oglethorpe—*Oglethorpe*, by L. F. Church, and *James Edward Oglethorpe, Imperial Ideal-*

ist, by A. A. Ettinger—have been published in the last ten years.

On January 13, 1733, there arrived at "Charles Town," South Carolina, the two-hundred-ton ship "Ann," completing a voyage of seven weeks from England with 110 persons on board. The ship was welcomed by the high officials of the colony of South Carolina, with promises to aid the newcomers in getting settled in the new country.

The heartiness of the welcome may seem a little surprising when we learn that the newcomers were to found a colony on territory then belonging to South Carolina. There was nothing secret about the new enterprise. In the eighteenth century England was well served by a competent press which sent its publications to the American colonies by every boat. In addition, the Charles Town officials had been amply informed by the governmental authorities of England just who the newcomers were and what they were to do.

The leader of the enterprise was James Edward Oglethorpe, of whom any well-informed person in Charles Town had already heard much and was soon to hear more. We leave the newly arrived travelers for a while to tell somewhat about Oglethorpe; for the more we know of him, the more we shall understand the people whom he brought with him.

James Edward Oglethorpe was born on December 22, 1696, of distinguished parentage, with an ancestral line which industrious and careful genealogists have traced back through six centuries. His father, Theophilus Oglethorpe, was a devoted follower of James II and was driven out of England in the "Glorious Revolution" of 1688, but somehow managed to win a place in the House of Commons in spite of his Jacobite sympathies, holding a seat from Haslemere, which his son James Edward afterward held. The Jacobite sympathies of Theophilus Oglethorpe were as nothing compared with those of his wife, Eleanor Nall, a maid at the court of Charles II in attendance on Louise, Duchess of Portsmouth. The ancestry of Eleanor was worthy enough, but she had more than ancestry to rely on. There have never been any reflections upon her character, except her loyalty to the exiled James II after William III had come to the throne of England. It will be remembered that it was this same James II to whom Susannah Wesley was so devoted that she would not say "Amen" when her husband Samuel prayed for the welfare of William.

To return to Eleanor. Her experience at court circles taught her just about all there was to know in those eighteenth-century days concerning place hunting and place finding, and that was a great deal. She was an apt learner. She was always busy trying to "place" Jacobites—indeed, kept up dubious connections between the court which James tried to maintain on French soil after 1688 and sympathizers in high position in England.

James Edward was given whatever training he was willing to receive at Eton and Oxford. There was enough of Jacobitism at Oxford to make young Oglethorpe feel thoroughly at home and to keep alive his sympathies with the restless and conspiring Eleanor. His name appears to have been dropped from the Oxford rolls in 1717 and turns up in a troop of guards under Marlborough. Next he appears in service with Prince Eugene. He was under fire at the Battle of Belgrade in 1717. By 1719 he was back in England where he became the head of the family estate at Westbrook. Not much is known of him until 1722, when he won a seat in Parliament from Haslemere.

His career in Parliament did not begin auspiciously. His election was contested because he did not get a majority of votes cast, though he did have a plurality. The contest was dropped, however. Oglethorpe seems to have been a fiery young soldier, with the standards of honor accepted by eighteenth-century warriors. On one occasion when "overcome with wine" he got into a quarrel with a "linkman," who beat him over the head, whereupon Oglethorpe retaliated by inflicting upon his assailant injuries which resulted in death.

I wish I could say that somewhere about this time the young Oglethorpe passed, like so many others of his generation, through a marked spiritual crisis which changed his view on life. There is no record of such a change except in his conduct, but there was complete enough change there. What we do know is that about a year after entering Parliament, Oglethorpe began the advocacy of measures, all of them humanitarian, all of them broad-minded, all of high moral quality, all with a touch of utopianism, all animated by religious motive.

We mention in passing a minor interest of Oglethorpe, though I do not know that it bears directly on the Georgia enterprise. I refer to his work in behalf of the seamen in the English navy. The treatment of seamen has until quite recent times been an almost unrelieved horror. On board ship the captain is the absolute monarch. His word is law. Disobedience in other days might mean punishment almost to death. Here too it was said that the ship owners and the ship captains could not choose their human material but had to rely upon the press gang. I have myself talked with American sea captains who had to "shanghai" their crews—that is to say, get them drunk and have them kidnaped and carried aboard ship, outward bound to heaven knows where. Those who get irritated over the demands of sailors' trade unions in our day ought to take a little time to look into the condition of English and American sailors aboard ship in Oglethorpe's time—and in later times, for that matter

—when the rope's end was the symbol and instrument of the authority of captains and ship owners. Only those so incurably romantic that they are blind to human dignity can prate of the joys of the seaman's life in the days of Oglethorpe. It is to the lasting credit of Oglethorpe that from the beginning to the end of his parliamentary career he never lost sight of the needs of English seamen.

We come now to Oglethorpe's interest in, and aid to, poor debtors. It requires only a little knowledge of English social history to recall the frightful jail treatment given in England to debtors who could not pay their financial obligations. We today look back upon jail sentences for debt as punishments of a dark age, but they seemed reasonable enough at the time. The English knew as well as any people that putting a man in jail would not put money in his pocket; but they counted on the generosity of relatives, or friends, or generously disposed humanitarians, to come to the help of the imprisoned debtors. The tradition is that the jewels of Susannah Wesley were used to help her husband Samuel out of jail. Readers of *Pickwick Papers* will recall the descriptions of life for debtors in Fleet Street Prison—and that at a long period after Oglethorpe's day.

It is easy for us at this late date to bear down too heavily on what we think of as the brutality of England in the eighteenth century. There was brutality aplenty, but some of it was hardly avoidable. Unemployment in that century was widespread. Men walked the streets because they had nothing to do and no place to go. Naturally they fell into thievery. We shall see in a moment that Oglethorpe had a constructive plan for dealing with them. John Howard is entitled to everlasting praise for his work in improving the conditions of England's prisons, and won indeed unstinted eulogy from John Wesley, who in his ministry learned much about English prisons; but the approach of Howard and that of Wesley were both palliative. Oglethorpe was the first outstanding citizen of England to make constructive suggestions in this field and to set to work a positive plan.

The beginning of the Georgia experiment was in this wise. Out of his realization of the hopelessness of the plight of debtors in English prisons, Oglethorpe dreamed his dreams of a colony in America which would give such unfortunates not only a haven but a new chance. A man named King, in business in London on a small scale, left £15,000 to three trustees to be used for charitable purposes. One of the trustees was an heir of the maker of the will and sought to secure the funds for himself. Through Oglethorpe's services the heir's selfish plan was defeated and the other trustees voted £5,000 of the estate to Oglethorpe's colonization plan. That was the beginning. The additional sum of £900 came from another estate of which Oglethorpe was a trustee. More important than these funds themselves was the fact that John, Viscount Percival, afterward Earl of Egmont, became a trustee of the Georgia enterprise. After Oglethorpe, Egmont was the most forceful figure in the Georgia movement, though Egmont rendered his service for the office of the trust in London.

We come back now to the little group of 110 disembarking from the "Ann" at Charles Town. They were to join their leader in creating a colony from the ground up. The geographical limits of the new colony seem at first to have been indefinite. South Carolina was supposed to reach from Spanish territory on the southeast to French territory on the northwest. Georgia was to be between the Altamaha and Savannah rivers. The first task was to carry out the orders of the charter for the founding of Savannah, to be built on five thousand acres about ten miles from the mouth of the Savannah River. The site was on high ground overlooking the river, with a pleasant "landskip," according to Oglethorpe.

Here was Oglethorpe's problem set for him, and a pretty problem it was. It is difficult to watch Oglethorpe's career in Georgia from beginning to end and not realize that the higher philanthropic and moral motives were with him predominant. Yet no man who has ever embarked on a scheme at all utopian has done

so with a more complete practical talent than Oglethorpe. He had to conquer natural obstacles and human obstinacies and inadequacies of resources. It
would be hard to find his equal for sheer dogged per-
sistence in carrying his plan through, and for patience
in the midst of indescribable trials. Suppose we glance
at a few of the difficulties: the keeping of his people
in fair temper, people whose prison experiences had
not notably developed their capabilities or their "dis-
positions"; the guarding against occasion for jealousy
on the part of South Carolina, which while welcoming
the founding of the new colony nevertheless was uncer-
tain as to just what some features in Georgia's charter
meant, especially as to whether the control of military
resources in Georgia was to be in the hands of South
Carolina officials; the amicable treatment of the Indians; the avoidance so far as humanly possible of
disagreements with the Spaniards in Florida, who
claimed all the territory into which Oglethorpe had
come. In addition there was trouble from the outset
over what was called "tail male"—the reckoning solely
by the male line—in the inheritance of land. Once
more, Oglethorpe had to satisfy the trustees of the
Georgia fund back in London as to the progress of the
enterprise. The Georgia trustees were like all others
of their kind. They never could see that if Oglethorpe
was to get anything done in Georgia he would not have
much time for correspondence. He does not seem

ever to have been given to much writing. How could he have been? During all his Georgia career he had only himself on whom to rely. None of his helpers were of much value. His government had to be strictly personal. He had to know every man, woman, and child in the community. He had to listen to everybody who thought it necessary to say anything.

It is entirely credible that nobody among the earlier settlers in Georgia in Oglethorpe's company was much concerned with philanthropy. Of course it was not to be expected that the neighbors of Savannah would be overjoyed at the coming of prison time servers, though there quickly came to be more in Oglethorpe's plans than the relief of debtors. The distress of soul caused by Oglethorpe's knowledge of English prisons was the initial emotional and moral stir which sent him to Georgia, but his purposes for helpfulness to his fellow men soon reached out beyond that.

The motives which led to the founding of Georgia were mixed, not so much in this or that individual mind as in the aims of different groups. Those officials who welcomed Oglethorpe at Charles Town on his first arrival were not happy, chiefly over the humanitarian purposes of the new colony founder. They were interested because they knew Parliament and England were interested, and they were confidently counting on new resources to help protect them from Indians and

Frenchmen and Spaniards. The higher aims Oglethorpe had to cherish for his own guidance.

Oglethorpe once said of himself that he had no desire to be a Don Quixote, by which he no doubt meant that he had no notion of trying to found an ideal commonwealth without the most complete reliance upon practical instruments. It is for this yoking of high moral purpose with practical expedients that his enterprise was notable. At the outset, indeed, there was nobody to interfere with him, though interference came fast and often later on. There are two elements in any moral effort—the devotion to the ideal in itself and the persistent and uncompromising search for ways and means of carrying out the ideal. It is probably to the credit of human nature that we are so made that our admiration flows most spontaneously to the man who stands by the ideal through thick and thin regardless of consequences, who will stand by the ideal though the heavens fall. It has been often observed, however, that the moral devotion which brings down the heavens through slighting the practical is not altogether desirable. It has taken too long and cost too much to get the heavens up, for one thing. Perhaps those who read about Don Quixote, the Knight of the Sorrowful Figure, think that Cervantes put Sancho Panza into the romance as a foil, to bring out the higher qualities of the knight by suggesting the earthy commonplaceness of his squire. This misses an essential, namely, that the earthy, dusty, and muddy good sense of Sancho was often wiser than the lofty romantics of his master.

In March, 1734, Oglethorpe went back to England on business for the colony. He left behind him eleven communities well on the way toward at least a degree of prosperity. This first period of Oglethorpe's career in Georgia is pronounced by competent students to have been the most successful, though as always a good deal depends here upon the standards of success.

Suppose we look at some achievements or attempts during this period.

First, the Indian problem. Of course we have to look at this from the background of the times. The people of the eighteenth century were proud to think of their century as the century of reason. There was, however, quite as much sentimentalism in the air in that century as in any. We admit that just at this time not much was being said about the "noble red man"; but there was considerable unrealistic sentimentalism going, nevertheless, by which I mean a glorification of the Indian without much realization that in actually dealing with him his helpers had to take him where they found him and as he was.

We have two contemporaries of Oglethorpe who expressed pronounced views on the Indians, George Berkeley and John Wesley. A moment's consideration of the attitudes of these two will help us to see some of the superior soundness of the opinions and policies of Oglethorpe. Oglethorpe consulted with both Berkeley and Wesley on the best methods of dealing with Indians. The question here is profoundly important; for although the policy toward the North American Indian is not so vital now as in earlier days, the relation of the so-called more favored peoples of the world to the less favored is of larger consequence today than ever before in the world's history. The most attractive biography of Oglethorpe refers to him in the title as an idealistic imperialist. In his own day Oglethorpe saw farther and deeper into the problems of imperialism than any other man of his time, and in no realm was his insight surer than in that of the obligations of the more favored peoples to those not so favored.

George Berkeley, in the first rank of the world's philosophical idealists, was a friend of the Earl of Egmont and desired to go to the Indies as a missionary —by Indies including the colonies on the American mainland. Egmont worked long to secure financial help for Berkeley, but with no large success, though Berkeley did go to Rhode Island and lived there for three years, awaiting Parliamentary grants for his educational plans for the Indians which never came. Berkeley sang of America as

The seat of innocence,
Where nature guides and virtue rules.

25

After Berkeley had returned to England he met Oglethorpe repeatedly, and Oglethorpe convinced him that the responsibility for aiding the natives of America was not to be met by colleges. Berkeley seems by then to have given up his hope of missionary work in America and lent whatever support he could command to the furtherance of Oglethorpe's Georgia project. Oglethorpe was one of the best friends the North American Indian ever had, but he was not ready to seek to uplift the Indian by colleges, nor presumably by the Berkeleian idealism.

To get the attitude of John Wesley we have to run a few steps ahead of our narrative. John Wesley came out to Georgia, sailing in October, 1735, with Oglethorpe on the second trip. He expected to labor among the Indians and was grievously disappointed when he found that he must devote his pastoral attentions to the English.

Wesley made the same mistake others have made of thinking of uncivilized man as innocent of all sophistication, with his mind like a clean slate—what John Locke would call a *"tabula rasa"*—white and stainless for the simple and glad reception of the Gospel. There had not been much careful, not to say scientific, study of Indian life and culture in those days, or Wesley would have known that the slate of the Indian's mind was not clean by any means, but that through hundreds of generations Indian tribes had been trained to a distinctively Indian spiritual fiber. Something soon changed in Wesley's attitude toward the Indians. He pronounced them murderers, adulterers, thieves, and almost everything elese he could lay his tongue to. According to him, they would sit on the bank of a stream and look at the stream, and then at the sky, and then at one another. It must have been a strain on John Wesley to see anybody sitting down at all, and vacant staring he could not comprehend.

Now Oglethorpe took the Indians about as they were. At the outset he looked upon them as human beings to be treated as such. He did not, however, regard the Indians as the only human beings in America, with rights above those of all other human beings. Every now and again some romanticist proclaims that by right this land belongs to the American Indians, and that presumably everybody else should forthwith get off the continent or be evicted for trespass. Oglethorpe did not believe that; but he did believe that the Indians had rights as human beings and as dwellers on American soil, and that these rights should be respected. If his spirit could have been imitated in other colonies, more than a full century of dishonor could have been avoided. There were other colonial policies more decisive than his, as that of Underhill in New England, who threw a lighted torch into an Indian stockade and burned to death eight hundred in one night. Underhill's conscience was of tougher texture than Oglethorpe's.

Fair dealing was the secret of Oglethorpe's success with the Indians, and he was successful. He would not conclude a deal with an Indian before the Indian understood it. He would not show any impatience with an Indian. He would bestow as much care upon a sick Indian as upon a sick white man. The result was that he never lost his hold upon the Indians as long as he had any measure of control in Georgia. The Indians willingly ceded to him the land on which Savannah was built, and never uttered a syllable of regret. Under Oglethorpe the Indians showed qualities which Wesley never detected. On his return to England after his first trip he took Tomochichi, an Indian chief, with him. Under Oglethorpe's kindliness the chief responded with a delicacy of appreciation for all favors shown him which astounded some of the most expert connoisseurs of correct behavior in England.

The first years in Georgia were devoted largely to putting a sound economic foundation under the colony. There were already in the New World types of economic activity which were troubling Oglethorpe, such as the wrongs perpetrated by traders with the Indians. Oglethorpe always tried to find a substitute for activities of which he did not approve. From the beginning he tried to introduce silk culture into Georgia and succeeded so well with it that he sent to England enough

28

silk for the making of a dress for the Queen—a dress which she was proud to wear. The silk industry did not last long. It was later displaced by tobacco culture. I mention the silk industry to indicate Oglethorpe's resourcefulness.

The first years, hard as they were, were easier than the period covered by the second visit to Georgia. Without Oglethorpe's presence some of the colonists had fallen afoul of one another. Thomas Causton, the storekeeper, was a worthy man in many respects, but a troublemaker. Moreover, he could never keep his accounts straight; and though he was to all reports intentionally honest, his inaccuracies were of themselves such as to set a community by the ears. The second trip across had been severe, with fearful storm. The only passengers on board who seemed to be in full control of themselves were a group of Moravian immigrants. Two women who turned out to be adventuresses filled the ears of John and Charles Wesely with stories of improper relations with Oglethorpe, stories to which the Wesleys would not have listened for a minute if they had been just a bit more sophisticated. There is no indication that Oglethorpe dealt at all harshly with the Wesleys. Probably in his understanding of almost everybody he met he understood the Wesleys also, perhaps much better than they understood themselves. Charles was the more trying of the two. He had come out to be Oglethorpe's secretary, but evidently assumed that he was somewhat above such work. It ended as such cases usually do—in somebody else's doing the work. Here the somebody else was John.

Probably the greatness of Oglethorpe's character comes out quite as clearly in standing steady in the midst of scandalous gossip as at any other time. After the second arrival the talebearing and tattling and backbiting never ceased. It followed Oglethorpe till long after he had left Georgia never to return. The marvel is that Oglethorpe did not become embittered or disillusioned. He did not have to go to Georgia. He went of his own accord—and largely at his own expense, for when his relation to Georgia was over it appeared that he had advanced a sum total of his own money amounting to $450,000 or £90,000. Yet his idealism never failed, though he said but little about it. We note that after a time he ceased to encourage the English to come to Georgia, and welcomed most heartily immigrants from continental Europe. This is not to be taken as too serious a reflection on the debtors whom Oglethorpe brought with him. Oglethorpe took only those who had the consent of their creditors. Still this type of colonist is not the highest. Even though Samuel Wesley, the father of John and Charles, had served a term in a debtor's prison, we are not to suppose that the most of the debtors were of Samuel's stamp. All debtors had felt at least a touch of defeat.

Having felt the world's rough hands, they were not eager to find that hand still rough in the new land.

Georgia provided a refuge also for some immigrants from continental Europe. Before Oglethorpe had got far into the Georgia project, he had become interested in the persecuted Salzburgers in Austria, where Protestants by the thousands had been so harshly treated that they had fled to England and Holland. As soon as he took hold of the Georgia scheme, therefore, he was responsive to the suggestion that Salzburgers be allowed to accompany him to Georgia. The Salzburgers preferred to live in Georgia pretty much by themselves and in their own way. Their persecutions had come out of their loyalty to religious convictions, a fact which necessarily made a difference between them and those who had suffered chiefly because they could not pay their debts.

At any rate, Oglethorpe's welcome of the Salzburgers was not only a noble piece of philanthropy in itself but a stroke of sound policy. So far as he could, Oglethorpe was determined to have the right settlers for Georgia. He would do the best he could for all who might be in Georgia without his choosing them, but his choices where he could choose at all were of the best. Hence it came about that he welcomed not only the Salzburgers but the Moravians as well. The famous Count Zinzendorf personally asked Oglethorpe to accept Moravians as colonists in Georgia, a request which Oglethorpe readily granted.

Before Oglethorpe finally left Georgia, the permanent settlers included members of the Church of England, Salzburgers, Moravians, and Scottish Highlanders. Oglethorpe himself seems to have been hospitable also to Jews, though the other colonists did not make them welcome. By understanding with the governmental authorities in England, Roman Catholics were not accepted.

It is thus clear that Georgia soon came to be not merely a relief to poor debtors but a refuge for those persecuted for religion. One is tempted to think of the Puritan fathers and their settlement of Massachusetts as one reads of Oglethorpe. To be sure, Massachusetts had back of it a hundred years of experience when Oglethorpe came to Georgia—experience by which Oglethorpe could profit. Moreover, the struggles for the conquest of the new land were incomparably harder in New England than in the colony to the south. Perhaps no such iron rule and discipline were necessary in Georgia as in the North. Still, in some respects Oglethorpe shows to advantage in comparison with the Puritan settlers. Certainly he made more place for liberty of conscience than was made in the North. Certainly, too, he made more allowance for personal liberty in the individual's own affairs than did the Massachusetts rules. It would be a stiff task to free the Puritan from the charge of probing and prying into his neighbor's concerns. Tragedy always seems to overshadow the Puritan settlements; but while there was tragedy enough in any American colony in the eighteenth century, the social and cultural atmosphere in Georgia appears to have been more genial than in New England.

Georgia needed both the Salzburgers and the Moravians, but they could not have been the easiest neighbors to get along with. It was a wise insight which prompted these stern Protestants—Calvinists, for that matter—to ask for allotted villages for themselves. Egmont called the Moravians enthusiasts who thought that whatever came into their minds came straight from the Lord. All who knew them in Georgia, however, unite in praising them. Without intending to raise questions as to economic implications, Charles Wesley commended the Moravians as the "cheapest" workers in Georgia. Wesley meant to praise the Moravians for working for less pay than any others in Georgia; but it is not pleasant to read this ominous note, prophetic of coming eras of long hours and low standards of living and scanty pay. Still, there was no especial danger of wrong to the Moravians themselves. They were a sturdy set, rejoicing in work as an ordinance of God. They were so sure that they were at all times receiving messages from God that they did not care overmuch about anything that men said or thought. Georgia treated the Moravians well, indeed gave them their start in the new world. They were, however, conscientious objectors to war, absolutists as we would call them today. When Georgia began to grow into significance as a colony, Oglethorpe had to ask his colonists for military service. Thereupon the Moravians departed for Pennsylvania—another long, stern journey for the sake of conscience.

Oglethorpe was a soldier—he had been trained as a professional soldier. We do not require much imagination to see Oglethorpe's perplexity at pacifism as extreme as that of the Moravians. We live two hundred years later than Oglethorpe, and we have not even yet come far in thoroughgoing appreciation of such pacifism as that of the Moravians. No word of perplexity, certainly none of impatience, escaped Oglethorpe's lips. There was sturdy worth in the conduct of the Moravians in leaving Georgia. They desired above all else to keep unsullied their conviction of nearness to God, and they were not willing to accept the support and protection of a colony for which they would not bear arms.

Oglethorpe never could have accepted the point of view of the Moravian conscientious objectors; but he did take some positions which must have seemed equally "enthusiastic," even fanatical, to the English in Georgia. One was his opposition to the liquor traffic. Oglethorpe had no objections to ale and beer and wine, but he fought rum. He felt that he could not lead the colony to any worth-while success if rum was to abound. In this he was moved by his consciousness of responsibility for the Indians. Here again we come upon the farsightedness in the statesmanship of this leader. The so-called civilized lands have always insisted that they have had a right to sell to natives in noncivilized lands whatever those natives would pay for. Two centuries ago Oglethorpe stood for the doctrine of the trusteeship of the so-called favored peoples for the less favored. The white man has concocted deadly liquors, which must not be used for the degradation of natives of so-called backward lands. Edmund Burke was the first great Englishman to preach a similar doctrine of responsibility; but a generation before Burke, Oglethorpe was applying the idea of trusteeship to a backward people while winning that people to acceptance of his leadership.

From the beginning of the third sojourn of Oglethorpe in Georgia he began to meet the play of economic forces which nullified much of the good he had begun. There was the trouble among the traders with the Indians. Not that there were any considerable numbers of such traders in Oglethorpe's own groups, but the colony of Georgia had colonial neighbors who had no high notions of the rights of Indians. Trade with Indians has always called forth frontiersmen of the least desirable quality and brought out their worst features. That the Indian desired in exchange for precious furs only trinkets of the least value to the white man, or—worse still—rum or firearms, made for desperate exploitation of the Indians. A trader among Indians once said to me that in criticism of such traffic we must always remember that traders do not go forth into the lands of Indians for their own health, or the health of the Indians. This same man told me that once an Indian in a company of white traders on a fur-gathering expedition lost his mind, and that when the poor demented red man became too heavy a burden to carry to a settlement, the white men, of whom my acquaintance was one, forthwith shot him. This was within the period of my own lifetime. It is not likely that traders' methods two centuries ago were much better. The English and French and Spaniards in southern North America were all anxious to make the most for themselves out of the rich Indian fur trade. Oglethorpe's attempts to control the trade by license soon came into collision with these other national groups, to say nothing of South Carolina.

Still wider, indeed world-wide, economic forces were coming upon the stage. We cannot say that economic forces are the sole or even the chief social powers, but their influence is enormous. Take the relation of Georgia to the West Indies. Georgia had abundance of tall, straight pine trees, most desirable for building; the West Indies, its nearest overseas neighbors, had molasses and rum. The possibility of cutting down and shipping trees, which cannot all be used at home, and getting therefor rum, which can be made almost an article of currency, is perennially attractive even to those who have no intention of drinking the rum themselves; to the rum drinkers of Georgia, the restrictions on the potent liquor seemed to be the closing of a door to the quickest psychological way out of the hardships and monotony of pioneer life. During the terrible depression that began in 1929 a foremost publicist in the United States urged the loosening of the laws against the liquor traffic on the plea that during bad times people need some psychological escape from the hardness of their lot. The demand for alcoholic beverages in frontier conditions has never been adequately recognized in its psychological aspects—the demand for intoxicating drinks because they are intoxicating, or because, as the Englishman in India used to say, they supply the quickest passage out of India.

Then there was negro slavery of world-wide importance. All around Georgia in Oglethorpe's time slavery had become an established institution, a vested interest. It had flourished in the South American colonies for over a hundred years. It seemed to be a providential agency for the agricultural development of tropical lands. Even Oglethorpe's loyal Salzburgers asked him for slaves. George Whitefield, who had come into Georgia just after John Wesley had left, wanted slaves for his work at the famous Bethesda

Orphanage, to which he gave so much of his time and strength. It is not likely that in Georgia's earliest days slavery had taken on the evils of those later peculiarities which Fanny Kemble so graphically described, but the main outlines of what slavery was to be were already discernible before Oglethorpe finally left.

In his attempts at creating a utopia Oglethorpe's work failed. In 1750 the antislavery clause was repealed, and two years later Georgia had become a crown colony.

Oglethorpe's failures, if so they may be called, were due partly to the fact that his colony had neighbors. South Carolina was one, with liquor being smuggled across the border and with all the frictions inevitable when a slave state is next door to a free state. The other neighbors were Spanish possessions and French possessions. It was due to Oglethorpe's own military efforts that Spain did not get possession of all the territory of Georgia, and possibly of much besides. Without attempting to justify the imperial methods of conquest in the eighteenth century, we must admit that it is an incalculable blessing that Oglethorpe won as a soldier where he failed as a philanthropist.

After Georgia became a crown colony it was caught in the current of British imperial policies. Sir John Seeley once said that Britain became an empire in a fit of absence of mind. There is not much to warrant this judgment. In all her colonies Britain worked assiduously for her own policies. The Navigation Acts cannot be characterized as conceived in a fit of absence of mind, unless perhaps we mean absence of the highest type of mind. As a last word, let it be said that the imperialist Oglethorpe rose far above his contemporaries at Whitehall in his conceptions of what the British Empire should be. He was above all playing of special favorites. He held to the doctrine of imperial interdependence, with all members working together for the good of the whole—an anticipation of a commonwealth of nations on the one hand and a moral trusteeship for backward peoples on the other. Much of the criticism of Oglethorpe after his work got well going was just the clash of his ideals with the practical expedients of a commonplace order of statesmanship.

It is a pleasure to know that Oglethorpe lived to an advanced age with an increasing recognition of his moral worth by all sorts and conditions of men. It is not easy to please such diverse types of characters as Salzburgers, Moravians, Scottish Highlanders, and American Indians; yet Oglethorpe achieved this marvel. Dr. Samuel Johnson had for Oglethorpe, long a member of the Johnson circle, unqualified admiration, also such respect for him that he never attempted to tread upon him with any of the heavy-footed Johnsonese sarcasm which at times so closely resembled intellectual and moral bullying—and this respect Ogle-

thorpe heartily reciprocated. John Wesley, who in
Georgia worried himself and annoyed Oglethorpe over
his inability to get from Oglethorpe a statement of religious experience fully to the Wesley liking, freely
extolled the goodness and greatness of Oglethorpe's
soul. Oglethorpe and Wesley met at a social circle in
the last days of the former's life. Oglethorpe seized
Wesley's hand and kissed it as a supreme mark of
honor. Perhaps we had better stop here with that picture before us.

JOHN WESLEY

JOHN WESLEY came to America as a minister of
the Church of England in Georgia in 1735 and remained till 1737. After Methodism had got well
a-going in England he sent preachers to America from
1770 till the formal organization of the Methodist Episcopal Church in 1784. Through these he kept a measure of control in the growth of Methodism in America.
By the time he died in 1791 he had so well laid down
the essentials of Methodist procedure and teaching that
he had determined the course of a main stream of
American religious life for generations to come.

What did Wesley bring with him on his journey
to Georgia? Chiefly he brought himself—a deeply
religious spirit, a mind well trained by the best educational opportunities in England, an iron will with unusual power of enforcing itself on others. He brought
with him his father's approval, his mother's affectionate
sanction likewise, and the good wishes of many good
English churchmen who cherished large expectations
as to the material as well as the spiritual success of
Oglethorpe's enterprise.

It has been said so often that Wesley's work in Georgia was not a success that the notion that Wesley
failed there is quite a general assumption. This as-

sumption comes largely out of a perhaps unconscious comparison of what Wesley achieved in Georgia and what one thinks he ought to have achieved through the spiritual powers which he afterward revealed. He did not have those powers in Georgia—they were developed out of experiences through which he had not then passed! George Whitefield arrived in Georgia shortly after Wesley had returned to England. He must have heard just about all the criticisms likely to be current in Savannah, a small town of only a few hundred people. Whitefield knew Wesley as well as any one at the time knew him and he soon saw what he had done. It was his expressed judgment that Wesley's work had been successful.

In all opinions as to success and failure we must first ask what was possible. Wesley came to America to labor among the Indians. That proved at once to be out of the question. He was imperatively needed for work among the Europeans. Those for whom he was thus assigned the religious responsibility were Englishmen, many of them poor debtors released from prison that they might go to Georgia; Salzburgers, devotedly pious but not at all English in intellectual or religious outlook; Moravians, stiffly set in their own ways; Highland Scots, excellent human material but not of the most malleable quality. Into such a variegated assortment of religious beliefs and practices came Wesley—High-Church, prelatic, Tory, inclined to be an ecclesi-

astical martinet. For effective religious administration
a considerable degree of like-mindedness on the side of
the people is indispensable. And there must be notable
agreement between people and ministers to keep
ecclesiastical concerns moving at all pleasantly. We are
not to think of debtors cast into prison for unpaid
financial obligations as in quite the same class as
religious heroes persecuted for righteousness' sake.
Such unfortunates are hard to get along with. When,
therefore, Wesley insisted upon baptizing babies by
dipping them instead of by some milder method permitted by the church, he need not have been surprised
that his exactions did not increase his popularity.

Making all allowances for this overrigidity as to
ritualistic and liturgical rule, we may well believe that
Wesley's policy of strictness was justified. In frontier
communities, if there are to be churches at all, they have
to be uncompromising. A community set on the edge
of a wilderness, thousands of miles from its homeland
and hundreds of miles from any other groups of its own
kind, was in moral and spiritual peril as well as in physical danger. It would not do for the sentinels around
such a settlement to get too careless. In Georgia, Oglethorpe was shot at once at least, as was also Charles
Wesley. There were abundant possibilities of lawless-
ness. The moral and religious situation was at least
noticeably parallel to the physical situation. Wesley
saw in obedience to the church of Christ the guarantee

of individual and social uprightness. He knew what he was about in his extreme regularity. To be sure, that regularity fitted too closely into his own native methodicalness, but at the moment it was sound nevertheless. Some of the English complained that they had never heard of stiffness like that of John Wesley's religion. Probably not—but they had never been in a land like the American continent before, on a little strip of coast between three thousand miles of ocean on the one side and as vast a reach of savage wilderness on the other. The Georgia undertaking was not to be conceived of as a Maypole picnic. Indeed, the Moravians were just as stern with their people as was John Wesley with the English. Most likely the Moravians were more used to careful and thorough discipline than were the English. In looking at Wesley's sternness we must not forget that he greatly desired and sought for the religious freedom and joy at which the Moravians had manifestly arrived. An Englishman sent out to an uncivilized land to represent England maintains his own distinctiveness by observing the rules and etiquette of England. He will not surrender his own standards. He will not "go native." Similarly, Wesley would not yield by a hair's breadth in his convictions of what his religion called for.

While we are on this theme of Wesley's alleged overseverity, it may be just as well to reflect that other English colonies besides Georgia were severe in their religious exactions. For example, take Massachusetts and Connecticut. While the histories of these two colonies reach back a century farther than that of Georgia, there were severities aplenty in New England in Wesley's time. Wesley never attempted to set up a theocracy in Georgia. That is what the New England Puritans virtually did. Not that they succeeded—but they did work so effectively on the assumption that the voice of their ministers was the voice of God that they made the ministerial rule a burden grievous to be borne. Moreover, they went to such lengths of inquisitional prying into men's inner lives that they often violated all the proprieties and some of the elementary decencies. If any reader doubts this let him look through the records of some disciplinary procedures in Connecticut churches—let us say, confessions of secret misconduct exacted "before the congregation." In some records the chronicler adds more naïvely than innocently, "to the great gratification of the congregation." Wesley's ecclesiastical administration may have at times been annoying, but it never failed in high-mindedness. It may have been too far up in the air, but it never got down into the dirt.

Discussing the reasons for this alleged failure of Wesley in Georgia, there are those who find the answer simple and ready at hand in Wesley's statement that he went to Georgia to "save his own soul." Then, forgetting the change of emphasis a century later on the indications of salvation in a human soul—the change from search for the salvation of one's own soul to the search for the salvation, in the full sense, of others—they proceed to make out that Wesley in Georgia was in a most unworthy condition indeed. This is too summary. The outstanding religious classic in the popular opinion of Wesley's day, and before, was Bunyan's *Pilgrim Progress*. Bunyan's pilgrim never seemed to have any doubt as to whose soul he was seeking to save. This search by the pilgrim for his own salvation could not have been so very unworthy inasmuch as it inspired some of the deepest religious insights and some of the loftiest spiritual flights to be found in English literature. Seeking the salvation of one's own soul did not mean in Wesley's earlier days just the self-centeredness that the expression seems to suggest. The test in Wesley's time of an individual's salvation was his willingness, once convinced of his own salvation, to do all he could for the salvation of others. It makes a neat division of Wesley's life into periods to say that before America he sought his own salvation and after America the salvation of others, but the division is an oversimplification.

Georgia rendered Wesley service in helping him to a change from a view of Christian service as that of a servant of God to that of a son of God. Wesley's fault was not that he was seeking to save himself rather than others, but that he was counting on what he was doing as in itself of too much importance for either himself or for anyone else. First of all, he had to learn how little he could do by programs and schemes of religious exercises that did not reveal an attitude of free devotion. He had to learn that loyalty to God his Father which would do all possible for the divine kingdom without any too high estimate of value placed by the doer on the deeds themselves. It was the spirit of sonship revealed in the deeds that mattered. Practically speaking, Oglethorpe was acting in a more Christian fashion than Wesley, without apparently thinking much about it. He was not lecturing anybody, was rendering whatever service he could, not worrying over mistakes, making multifarious adjustments to manifold situations with a patience indescribable and illimitable. It is without doubt that he was acting as Wesley might have done if Wesley had been a little more spiritually mature. We do not know much about Oglethorpe's religious crises, but we do know that Wesley came to realize the fineness of his spirit and held him in highest honor in spite of the exactness and precision and scrupulousness with which Wesley himself insisted upon the observance of religious exercises.

Whatever faults Wesley himself had can be summed up in the word "immaturity." Though Wesley was well over thirty at the time of his Georgia experiences, he was altogether youthful in his religious practice and conduct. For example, any educational administrator who has had experience with young teachers knows that in their first attempts at teaching they set the standards for achievement by their pupils too high, especially if the instructors themselves are extremely conscientious. In giving examinations such instructors "mark" or "grade" too closely, with not enough "benefit of the doubt" to the student. Such an idealistic beginner may at first reject more than half his class as failures. Likewise with beginners in Christian pastoral guidance. Practically speaking, the requirements are likely to be too high. Georgia was Wesley's first real parish. He had been a faithful visitor upon unfortunates in prison during his days at Oxford but had really had no experience in parish tasks. The English in Georgia were far from ideal, but even in church affairs they knew a great deal. In the unfortunate differences which led to their seeking to hail Wesley into court for what was alleged to be injustice toward one of his parishioners, they showed remarkable knowledge of church law and procedure, though to Wesley's more exact familiarity with ecclesiastical rules and statutes only one or two out of the charges had any sound legal basis.

Though the entire setting of Wesley's life in Georgia was unusual, it could not be called abnormal. He passed through experiences there which were not without value to him later on. Georgia helped train and develop him in the directions which counted mightily in the leadership of the Methodist revival. Wesley was a capably trained scholar when he went to Georgia, but he did not then know much of the world of human beings "in the flesh." He did not know much about himself, as is indicated by his conduct in his first love affair—conduct irreproachable from the point of view of Wesley's intentions, but bungling from that of common sense. In that little community of about a thousand persons, with no books or newspapers, people just had to talk. What could be more interesting than the parson's love affair? To put the situation in Hibernian paradox, if the Wesley of Georgia could have been serving under the Wesley of organized Methodism in England, the older Wesley would simply have transferred the younger Wesley to some other circuit, and that would have been the end of it.

One little touch in Wesley's own narrative of the experience when his heart was "strangely warmed" may be reminiscent of Georgia. It will be recalled that after the quickening in Aldersgate, Wesley at once began to pray for his persecutors. The only enemies of Wesley of whom we know were those in Georgia. If the faces of the Georgia troublemakers passed before the memory of Wesley at Aldersgate, the fact was a remarkable instance of inconsequential agents as figuring consequentially in a crisis of transcendent importance.

John Wesley brought himself to America. He took back a greater self than he brought here.

We come now to the relation of Wesley to America in his relation to the Methodist workers. Methodists began to emigrate to America almost as soon as Methodism developed into a body of any considerable size in England. By 1766 a little handful of those who had come to New York started the enterprise known as John Street Church. Practically all who came between that date and the war of the American Revolution had had some contact with Wesley himself—Barbara Heck, Philip Embury, George Shadford, Joseph Pilmoor, Richard Wright, Thomas Rankin, Richard Boardman, Francis Asbury. Through most of this period Wesley appears to have regarded the Methodists in America as just so many Englishmen in America, with about the same conceptions of everything that dwellers in England had. It is likely that Wesley thought thus to the end of his life.

Wesley did not take the question of any organized work in America very seriously till the Bristol Conference in 1770. At that conference Thomas Rankin and Francis Asbury were sent out, to work wherever they could, about as they could. Rankin was more voluble than Asbury and produced more of an effect on Wesley, who knew Asbury only slightly. Rankin wrote back of what he might have done if he had possessed larger powers; and Wesley was almost persuaded, so that even after a year or more of successful work by Asbury, Wesley was on the point of recalling Asbury to England.

It will appear, I trust, before I finish this chapter, that the greatness of the contribution of Wesley to America was in his having prepared and led a religious movement for which historical events in America in the half century after 1760 prepared a continent-wide stage of action. Still, that religious movement, while it never would have succeeded as it did without the permanent stamp set upon it in England, had to be remolded in America in some essential details. Indeed, it was this remolding which made possible the preservation of the features most essentially English.

One good result of the American Revolution so far as Methodism was concerned was that it removed from America all the Methodist preachers who had originally come from England—except one, Francis Asbury, who proved to be the indispensable man.

Wesley's own attitude toward the American Revolution was not altogether surprising. When the revolutionary storm first showed signs of brewing, Wesley wrote most discriminatingly of the Americans, most appreciatively indeed. He told those in power in England what they could expect in a war with the colonies. There would be a long struggle, with hopes of English success not altogether rosy. As the months and years wore along, the lineaments of Wesley the

Methodist became fainter and those of Wesley the Tory sharper. Wesley's utterances and his attitude turned against America. There was not much that was original in his arguments; his dependence upon Dr. Samuel Johnson in the "Calm Address to the Americans" was quite evident. Wesley was not a political or an economic thinker or student. He was a close observer of English conditions as he rode up and down England. His remark that he knew more about England by personal contact than any other man alive was probably correct enough, but his political and social philosophy was Tory. He saw nothing wrong in the English mercantilism that would have kept the American colonies in political and economic dependence on, not to say bondage to, England forever, though he was always among the first to protest against manifest injustices by England toward her oversea dependencies. We remember that he spoke out against wrongs done by the English to the peoples of India.

Wesley had not place in his thinking for anything republican. Here we come upon a strange personal puzzle. Wesley taught and practiced the equality of all men before God. In his dealing with the least fortunate men, the least educated, the most hopeless so far as their circumstances were concerned, he was a democrat throughout. Though a Tory by temperament and conviction and training, he met every individual on a plane of equality so far as worth in the sight of God was concerned; yet the collective judgment of the masses even on a religious theme, to say nothing of a political or social question, weighed with him not at all.

Francis Asbury was English, but with a difference. From his arrival here he seems to have understood the Americans; at least, he made them understand him well enough to realize that he was heart, head, and hand one of them. By the accidental discovery of a letter which he attempted to send to England during the war, his complete loyalty to America was established; and though in the first years of the struggle he had to remain in obscurity amounting almost to concealment, in the later years he was allowed to continue his work about as he pleased. It has been remarked at times that in the history of Methodism the step from Wesley to Asbury is a step down. A step down from what to what? A step down possibly from one trained in the finest schools of England to one self-trained, but not a step down from a higher leadership to a lower so far as practical effectiveness was concerned. It is enough to say that Asbury did his work as effectively as Wesley did his and that neither could have done the work of the other.

It is easy to be unjust to Wesley for his attitude toward American Methodism. By the time the Americans had won their independence Wesley was eighty years old. When he wrote the "Dear Frankie" letter to Asbury—the letter in which he reproached Asbury for strutting as a bishop while he himself was content to be plain "Mr. Wesley"—he was over eighty, a fact which may measurably explain a peevishness at least resembling childishness. It is enough to say that Methodism was an essentially Wesleyan spiritual phenomenon, that it came to its widest activity on a stage provided and set by English standards of civilization and human values, that it had to be fitted to American points of view and ways of living if it was to act out the destiny set for it by historic world movements.

We may fittingly linger for a moment over a suggestion by Dr. H. B. Workman as to the significance of certain forces in English history which gave scope for American Methodism. Up to the middle of the eighteenth century the English colonies in America were hemmed in between the sea and the Allegheny mountains. Beyond the mountains were the French. The victories of the English armies, ending with the final one on the Plains of Abraham, freed the colonies for western expansion. A second momentous event at the turn of the century was the cession of the Louisiana Territory to the United States. Ironic as it may sound, one of Methodism's outstanding benefactors was Napoleon Bonaparte, who saw to it that the Louisiana Territory got into the hands of the United States. If it had not been for the victory of General Wolfe on the one hand and for Bonaparte's diplomacy on the other, Roman Catholicism might have been the ecclesiastical power of all the American continent west of the Allegheny Mountains, with a grade of civilization about like that of Quebec. There is further irony in the reflection that Bonaparte ceded the Louisiana Territory to the United States probably with the purpose of keeping the land out of the control of England, taking thus the surest path to securing the American continent for the English form of life and social organization!

Admittedly all such speculations are interesting. When a score of factors, each indispensable for a result, work together for the accomplishment of the result, each can claim the final credit. The situation is parallel to that of winning an election with a majority of one where a hundred votes were cast. Each one of fifty-one voters can claim that the victory is due to himself. Still, no matter as to the exact assessment of the forces at work in conquering the American continent for English civilization, the path was opened. With the dawn of the nineteenth century the doors of a continent were ajar for the fundamental principles of English institutions and culture.

It is altogether too easy to assume, after considerations like this, that the conquest of a continent is like the release of waters behind a dam, with the floods pouring forth in irresistible might. The spread of the English ideas and manners of life in America after

the War of Independence was more the putting forth
of the energies required for the taming of the thousands
upon thousands of square miles of land for new states
and cities. If we look merely at the physical force
required for subjugating the American continent in a
brief century, we shall probably have to call it the most
tremendous putting forth of physical energy ever
achieved in such a limited time. The work had to be
kept simple. At least at the beginning there was not
much chance for refinement. The working tools—
physical, intellectual, and moral—had to be reduced
to the straightest lines. The settlers from Europe had
left behind them much that they were willing to leave,
but they certainly found here only the barest rudiments
of anything. As a devout frontiersman put it, speaking
of what opportunities for education had been his: "I
know my A B C's, and I know my multiplication table,
and I know my Lord."

I am referring now to the task before Methodism in
what Theodore Roosevelt called the "winning of the
West." As will soon enough appear, these chapters
are not written in any mood of disparagement of any
other religious groups whatever; other groups in the
settlement of the country worked as hard and suffered
as much as, indeed more than, the Methodists. But I
am thinking of the sheer size of the task before the
Methodists—the sweep of length and breadth which

might have been paralyzing to the imagination if the imagination could adequately have seized them.

Confronted by such tasks, men act not so much out of definite plan as out of a movement of the total life which impels them in one direction rather than another. There were reasons why the Methodists had to make their chief fields the West. The more favored fields to the east had already been taken, and in those fields Methodism never won its decisive victories. New England had been a fairly stable society for a hundred years before Methodism was heard of in England, and both New York and Pennsylvania had likewise already long histories of social life and angles of view peculiarly their own. To the west and south lay the new lands.

Now if Methodism in America was to be limited to the eastern seaboard, its direction and control might have been left to Wesley and whoever was to succeed him to the leadership in England. New England and Virginia would have been pretty thoroughly English and would have supplied a narrow but somewhat important sphere for Methodism. At one time John Wesley seemed to think that if the Bishop of London would only take more interest in the churches of England in America by sending a bishop here, all the more pressing ecclesiastical needs could be met. When Methodists tried to get into Massachusetts, and Connecticut especially, they met an ecclesiastical resistance more gritty than pious.

The truth is that John Wesley, after the outbreak of the Revolution, never understood America. In this he is not at all to be blamed. Who in England at that time understood America? The Methodist preachers who had come out from England to America had almost all gone back, and their return revealed where their deeper interests lay. There was a trace of presumption in Wesley's taking for granted so completely his own overlordship of the Methodists in America. Not a score of preachers all told ever came from England to work in the colonies. A good deal is made in Methodist history of that famous Wesleyan conference at which Richard Boardman was sent forth to America and a collection taken for his expenses. The financial response was astonishingly generous, considering the resources of the preachers; but inasmuch as the total was but fifty pounds, the investment could not have laid Methodism in America under such a heavy debt to England as to lead to the expectation that American Methodism would follow the English very closely.

So after the Revolution the Methodists in America went their own way. They had to. It is from the massive necessities of the American religious situation that all the problems of American Methodism must be considered. How silly to waste time in talking about the validity of Wesley's ordination—whether "ordination" is the correct word or not makes not the slightest difference—in view of a chance to help lay the foundations of a new world. Wesley took the only wise course in the circumstances, though he seemed himself to be not altogether clear as to what he was doing, and Coke, one of the two men "ordained" or "consecrated" or "set apart"—whatever one wishes to call it—always seemed to suffer from a restless craving that some English bishop might grant him a ceremonial authorization a little more regular.

The situation in brief was this: providentially a field in America had been opened to English civilization; Methodism was a feature and phase of that civilization; Methodism was peculiarly fitted to carry forward its unique tasks; and while remaining true to its spiritual essentials, it had to adjust all ecclesiastical features to circumstances almost wholly new in the history of the Christian church. It is a high tribute to the character of the early American Methodists that they did as well as they did. They had firmly seized the essentials which had made Methodism a force in the world, and they refused to be bound by cramping precedents. The attempt was made in the closing years of Wesley's life to have him visit the Methodists of America. Possibly we may be thankful that the visit proved out of the question. Wesley would have been too old. He would have found himself in an environment strange to him; and though he would doubtless have been deeply gratified at the affectionate recognition heaped upon him, he would have felt the independence in the air. Yet if he could have seen deeply enough, and far enough, he would have seen that his own discoveries in Christian experience were to lead to the breaking of new light in the souls of millions of Americans yet unborn. He forged the instrument large enough and strong enough to lead in the spiritual subjugation of a continent.

In later chapters something can be said about one or more important debates on religious doctrine in America in the eighteenth century. Wesley's contribution to doctrinal interpretation was his defense of the character of God in the Calvinistic debate. For the purpose of the present chapter it is necessary to lay the stress on Wesley's teaching as to religious experience.

We must admit that everything that happens to a human being is human experience. The eighteenth century, however, sought not to expand the capacity of human experience but to limit it—to limit it to pure reason, or to as nearly pure reason as might be possible. Anything emotional was sensationalism.

Now there were many devout Christians in the England of Wesley's day who sympathized with this disparagement of emotionalism—Bishop Joseph Butler, for one. Butler's *Analogy* was heartily commended by Wesley as a piece of reasoning, with the reservation, however, that the *Analogy* would not mean much to the ordinary man. Wesley's Aldersgate experience, though not by any means the only instructive religious crisis through which he passed, reveals his attitude. Speaking of this experience, Wesley said that his heart was "strangely warmed," that he felt his sins had been forgiven, and that he began to pray for those who had badly used him. These terms are predominantly emotional. The expression "strangely warmed" can of course not be described, but it need not mean anything peculiar or queer. It may have meant a warming of heart strange to Wesley, an opening up of a side of his nature of which he had hitherto known little. He had come upon a new phase of experience.

It is obvious enough that throughout the history of the church the emotional element in experience has been indispensable and has determined wide currents of events. Nevertheless, periods of religious thought and practice undergo, or pass through, fashions. The eighteenth century was the era of the fashionable stress on pure reason. A fashion which sweeps the length of a century can develop marvelous power. The masses of the people during the eighteenth century were just as capable of emotional response as any, but they had not had the leadership which opened up the emotional possibilities. When Wesley began to open to his followers the channels of emotional expression, he not only found wide responsiveness but he also added a propelling power to the religious experience itself.

There is no wisdom or good sense in setting life in one of its fundamental activities over against another, as thinking over against doing, or either or both of these against feeling. Nevertheless, the thrill and tingle of life seems to be in the sensibility. Even the pleasures of what we call abstract reflection exist in the emotional glow which accompanies the stirring of the intellect. It is said of Isaac Newton that when he saw important mathematical formulations converging toward a significant conclusion he would become so excited that he could not himself finish the calculations. Intellectual effort which remains on the plane of the abstract does not attain to driving power. Personal reinforcements of spiritual energy through the marriage of thought with feeling are numberless. Nobody would be likely to select Immanuel Kant for any function save that of a thinking machine, but Kant's most quoted remark is that about the awe which held him as he gazed upon the starry heavens above or the moral law within.

Now Wesley knew how to arouse the feeling of men. He made them feel that religion was of primary concern. Whether he roused their response to a God of love, or brought them to a consciousness of freedom from sin or from enmity toward men, or helped them on toward a crisis which meant veritable new birth for them, he touched those nerves of sensibility where most of us live.

Wesley had also to deal with the question as to whether these experiences bore witness to any reality beyond themselves. In Wesley's century as in others before and after, the critic, not to say the cynic, sneered that feeling reveals nothing beyond itself—that, to use the more ponderous language, the feeling is subjective without any objective worth. Wesley stood firmly for the belief that, while a religious experience has value in its own right for the quality of the feeling itself, it points beyond itself; that it is caused by a reality beyond itself; and that its quality is a revelation of like quality in the object. It did not require much effort to bring men at all concerned about religion into the ventures of faith which led to an actual joy. Wesley's presentation was new, after the neglect of the churches to do more than proclaim abstract doctrine and urge limited rounds of church observances. The people responded in astonishing numbers, revealing a widespread religious hunger. The tendency to criticize early Methodism for crudeness, for emotional excesses, for "crowd contagion," has mostly passed. Wesley said that a religion that is not social is none at all. It would not be fair to say that he purposely made use of what we call "crowd contagion" for religious purposes, but he did recognize the value of this social force—the stimulus of the members of a group upon one another in an unconsciously collective spiritual effort. Methodist preachers did not know any such words as "escape mechanism," "complexes," and other such technical terminology; but they did know the psychological facts which today bear these scientific labels. Admitted that they, including Wesley himself, had no satisfactory theory to describe these phenomena, they did know fairly well how to deal with them, and guided many thousands of distracted minds to peace. "Integration" under their dealing became actual fact, though they did not call it that but stuck to the scriptural phrases "new birth" and "conversion."

No doubt there was much excess in the revival efforts of Methodism in America—and that too a score of years after such psychological uproar had ceased to be especially noticeable in English Methodism. The greater extremes of such expression and their longer continuance under American conditions were due mostly to the conditions themselves. Among the sacrifices asked of those who laid the foundations of civilization in continental America was that of living in situations in which most of the conventions and refinements of civilization were stripped off, leaving not much besides the rudiments of what could be called material civilized existence. If this could be kept in mind, it might lead to large modification of our judgment of the American followers of John Wesley. One of the marvels of American pioneer history is the degree to which the pioneer kept loyal to worthy political and moral and religious ideals. These men were seeking to accomplish in our vast continent in one century what it had taken England seven centuries to achieve, and until the nineteenth century they had no better tools for the work than the English had possessed.

There was plenty of room in pioneer America for all religious groups likely to appear. It now is evident that Methodism was soundly led in seeking out the "plain people," in holding before them certain elementary religious ideals, and in insisting upon these ideals with an intensity likely to be called narrow. Methodism, like other denominations, passed through its phases of narrowness, without which it might have disappeared. The best service the various denominations could serve in those early days was to develop each its own genius and its own loyalty. The hour of closer approach of the denominations to one another could come later.

Methodism took as its aim to "spread scriptural holiness throughout the land." Spreading implies making thin. Such work had to be extensive rather than intensive. There were in the settled parts of the United States at the time of the founding of the independent nation religious groups already prepared and measurably equipped to do intensive work. Take the problem of democracy. Much has been written of the development of religious organizations in the United States as an aid to democratic progress, though the influence has probably been quite as potent the other way round—democracy has influenced religious organizations too. Still the churches have served democratic progress mightily, though in various ways. The independent congregations, for example, served by making themselves autonomous democratic unities. It is sometimes urged that such entities in their relations to one another are ropes of sand. Nevertheless, the units are and have been vital, pouring streams of democratic power into the colonies. Some students have declared that it is questionable whether American independence could have been won if it had not been for the democratic spirit and technique worked out by the church organizations of New England.

Be that as it may, the Revolutionary War had been won before Methodism began to count for much in America. The Methodist Church was organized in 1784, during the decade when a constitution for the new republic was being wrought out. Methodist preachers must have heard plenty of debates over the proposed national constitutions. Not many of them had been long enough attached to any particular state to have imbibed deeply that mistaken state loyalty which so nearly wrecked the efforts of the constitution makers. The Methodist leaders thought from the first in terms of the new nation as a nation. Washington had but recently been inaugurated President of the United States when Bishop Asbury had begun making his long annual journeys from Maine to Florida, and thence to Kentucky, and thence back to the East. Incidentally, I may remark that at the time of his death in 1816,

Asbury had probably been seen by more persons in the United States than any other man ever had been, except Whitefield.

The first problem before Methodism, speaking of the organization, was that of the sheer extent of the country. When Asbury began his work as a bishop, Boston was nearly a week's journey from New York, and New York nearly two full days from Philadelphia. The distances to the points farther west were even longer, in terms of time taken for the journey. Ten days would have been good traveling from Philadelphia to Pittsburgh. Distances like these made spreading into a thin layer of denominational effort irresistible. To criticize such work as superficial is to miss the stupendous nature of the task and the gigantic heroism that could attack it.

We look again for an instant at Wesley's famous letter to Asbury in which he reproached the latter for allowing himself to be called "Bishop." There was a sound feeling back of Asbury's acquiescence in the use of the title. In the new land to the west there was little to suggest the importance of institutional religion. The people had to be led to take Methodism seriously. This depended first upon the compelling message of the preachers but next upon the impressiveness of the organizational features themselves. It was easy enough for Englishmen, and some Americans for that matter, to look amusedly at an episcopacy which consisted of two or three or four men traveling on horseback through an almost unbroken wilderness. The critics forgot that in England there was much to suggest the fact and importance of religion. A cathedral in an English town, venerable with three or four centuries of existence and service, was a silent witness to religion, and a witness of inescapable force. Whatever was to suggest religion in the American frontier had to be due to the faithfulness and energy of the leaders. These men had to build on foundations which in appearance did not suggest the titles which they bore. In that same famous letter Wesley chided Asbury for calling an institution a college when it could not have been more than a school. Wesley's criticism was sound enough from his own angle, but he knew nothing about the intentions and even of the prospects of the founders of the colleges. Some of these same so-called colleges came to be among the most significant educational forces in the land.

We can keep our perspective in studying the Methodists of America by remembering that they were among those in the vanguard in the conquest of a continent. They were stripped of all nonessentials for the warfare. In the meagerness of their equipment they appeared to be living on the fringes of civilization. They were indeed—but the fringes were the front fringes.

GEORGE WHITEFIELD

I SHALL attempt in this chapter to consider White-field as modifying, or perhaps softening, the ironclad Calvinism taught by Jonathan Edwards. This is admittedly a delicate task inasmuch as there is no reason to believe that Whitefield ever had any intention of exerting such an influence, or any suspicion that he was doing so. Whitefield's force in this respect was put forth indirectly and was due more to what he himself was than to anything he purposely said or did.

Before looking at New England Calvinism we mention some aspects of Whitefield's life and career which laid a basis for his effectiveness in the sphere of religious thinking. His early circumstances were very lowly and not especially promising for the development of religious leadership. His father died while White-field was a mere slip of a boy and the mother had to make a living by carrying on a tavern, where White-field's duty was to serve liquor to the customers. This did not mean in those days just what it would mean today. Whitefield's mother was a person of discernment and of energy. She made it possible for her son to get the preparatory training necessary for admission to college; and the boy himself found a position as servitor at Pembroke College, Oxford, where his tasks, though menial, were remunerative enough to make it possible for him to take all the courses required for his degree.

There still linger in the minds of readers about Whitefield two impressions which seem to date back to Oxford days. One of them is probably just—the impression that because of experiences as servitor at Pembroke he developed what the psychologist today delights to call an inferiority complex, which showed itself all through Whitefield's life in his deference to persons of social position and in his fondness for their company. Whatever the explanation, Whitefield did find gratification in being recognized by those of high position, especially by what he called "tiptop nobility." He allowed the Countess of Huntington to be his patron; and she possibly influenced him too much, though this must be qualified by the recollection that Whitefield made seven journeys to America and thus was much of his time beyond his patroness' reach. The Countess of Huntington was a dominating soul, of deeply genuine piety, of unusual robustness of mind, and of a not especially flexible will. By the way, there is a somewhat superficial judgment passed upon John Wesley that he was not strong in his dealing with women. There is enough in Wesley's career to make this opinion plausible; but over against it should be set the fact that Wesley did not allow any woman, or anybody else for that matter, to determine the course of early Methodism. The Countess of Huntington was entirely willing to tell how Methodist affairs should be conducted. She showed kindnesses to Wesley which Wesley accepted sparingly or not at all, never accepting invitations to her home readily and finding no noticeable satisfaction in the society he met there. Whitefield, it must be admitted, liked to be in the company of Chesterfield and Bolingbroke and of Sarah, Duchess of Marlborough, the wife of the great duke.

Conceding the pleasure which Whitefield evidently felt in the companionship of such society, let us not forget that this pleasure never caused him to swerve for an instant from his mission to the vast multitudes.

Another impression not at all just to Whitefield is that from his college days he was not a leader of any marked intellectual force. This may have been in a measure due to Whitefield's dramatic qualities as a speaker. From boyhood George Whitefield was an orator, and an orator of the actor stamp. It is easy to underestimate the intellectual force of the orator. It is true that the orator's eloquence rises to amazing heights and then dies down quickly, so that the critic declares that the orator's power is soon forgotten.

This applies equally to the actor. To be sure, the actor is speaking set lines; but even when his lines are forgotten, the overpowering revelation of a great mind in dramatic action is not forgotten. In my youth I heard my elders speak of the gifted actors of an earlier day—of Edwin Booth among men and of Rachel among women—all of them declaring that it would have been utterly impossible for anyone who had heard either Booth or Rachel with any degree of understanding ever to forget either. Now consummate acting requires intellect, and so likewise does genuine oratory. The content of lofty oratory may not of itself be especially weighty, but at a given moment in an ordinary idea may be given extraordinary velocity by the strength of the bow which drives the arrow. I remember hearing Whitefield called commonplace because of his preaching that every minister of the church ought to be a man converted, born again. That proposition was not commonplace when Whitefield was preaching. It was he who made it commonplace. As a discerning historian once said: "It was the extraordinariness of Whitefield's preaching that made the content of his sermons ordinary, commonplaces of universal acceptance."

Let us judge the quality of Whitefield's mind by its impact on three other minds. David Hume spoke with unqualified admiration of Whitefield's oratory, especially passages like the famous picture of the blind man just about to lose balance on the edge of a precipice. Jonathan Edwards and Whitefield were the closest of friends, though Edwards disapproved of the emotional excitement aroused in Whitefield's audiences and Whitefield took the criticism "coolly." Benjamin

Franklin esteemed Whitefield so highly that he once sought to persuade him to join in a virtual partnership in a semipublic enterprise with himself.

We must all admit that Whitefield's power as a preacher is not to be found in any utterances which have come down to us, taken by themselves. An old jibe is that Whitefield must have been eloquent indeed to make such utterances as his seem eloquent. Here, however, was his power—to make men see and act upon what ought to have been obvious to them.

I insert here an excerpt *Some Aspects of the Religious Life of New England* by George L. Walker, which in spite of its remarkable spelling is a lively and quickening description of the impression produced by Whitefield in New England.

Now it pleased god to send mr. whitfield into this land & my hearing of his preaching at philadelphia like one of the old aposels, & many thousands floocking after him to hear ye gospel and great numbers were converted to Christ, i felt the spirit of god drawing me by conviction i longed to see & hear him & wished he would come this way and i soon heard he was come to new york & ye jases [Jerseys] & great multitudes flocking after him under great concern for their Soule & many converted wich brought on my concern more & more hoping soon to see him but next i herd he was on long island & next at boston & next at northamton & then one morning all on a Suding about 8 or 9 oClock there came a messenger & said mr. whitfield preached at hartford & weathersfield yesterday & is to preach at middeltown this morning [1] at 10 o clock i was in my field at work i dropt my tool that i had in my hand & run home & run throu my house & bad my wife get ready quick to goo and hear mr. whitfield preach at middeltown & run to my pasture for my hors with all my might fearing i should be too late to hear him i brought my hors home & soon mounted & took my wife up & went forward as fast as i thought ye hors could bear, & when my hors began to be out of breath i would get down & put my wife on ye Saddel & bid her ride as fast as she could & not Stop or Slak for me except i bad her & so i would run until i was almost out of breth & then mount my hors again & so i did several times to favour my hors we improved every moment to get along as if we was fleeing for our lives all this while fearing we should be too late to hear ye Sermon for we had twelve miles to ride dubble in littel more then an hour & we went round by the upper housen parish & when we came within about half a mile of ye road that comes down from hartford weathersfield & stepney to middeltown on high land i saw before me a Cloud or fog rising i first thought off from ye great river but as i came nearer ye road i heard a noise something like a low rumbling thunder & i presently found it was ye rumbling of horses feet coming down ye road & this Cloud was a Cloud of dust made by ye running of horses feet it arose some rods into ye air over the tops of ye hills & trees & when i came within about twenty rods of ye road i could see men & horses Sliping along in ye Cloud like shadows & when i came nearer it was like a stedy streem of horses & their riders scarcely a hors more then his length behind another all of a lather and fome with swet ther breath rooling out of their noistrels in ye cloud of dust every jump every hors semed to go with all his might to carry his rider to hear ye

[1] The date was October 23, 1740.

news from heaven for ye saving of their Souls it made me trembel to see Sight how ye world was in a strugle i found a vacance between two horses to Slip in my hors & my wife said law our cloaths will be all spoiled see how they look for they was so covered with dust that they looked allmost all of a coler coats & hats & shirts & horses We went down in ye Streem i herd no man speak a word all ye way three mile but evry one presing forward in great hast & when we gat down to ye old meating house thare was a great multitude it was said to be 3 or 4000 of people asembled together we gat of from our horses & shook off ye dust and ye ministers was then coming to the meating house i turned and looked toward ye great river & saw the fery boats running swift forward & backward bringing over loads of people ye ores roed nimble & quick every thing men horses & boats all seamed to be struglin for life ye land & ye banks over ye river lookt black with people & horses all along ye 12 miles i see no man at work in his field but all seamed to be gone—when i see mr. whitfeld come up upon ye Scaffil he looked almost angellical a young slim slender youth before some thousands of people & with a bold undainted countenance & my hearing how god was with him every where as he came along it solumnized my mind & put me in a trembling fear before he began to preach for he looked as if he was Cloathed with authority from ye great god, & a sweet sollom Solemnity sat upon his brow & my hearing him preach gave me a heart wound by gods blessing my old foundation was broken up & i saw that my righteousness would not save me then i was convinced of ye doctrine of Election & went right to quareling with god about it because all that i could do would not save me & he had decreed from Eternity who should be saved & who not i began to think i was not Elected & that god made some for heaven & me for hell & i thought god was not

Just in so doing i thought i did not stand on even Ground with others if as i thought i was made to be damned my heart then rose against god exceedigly for his making me for hell now this distress lasted almost two years.[2]

In "action"—that is to say, in the actual delivery of a sermon—Whitefield was probably without a superior in the history of the English pulpit. He was made for the pulpit, and every movement in the pulpit enforced what he was saying. Everything about him was arresting; even his squint eye—possibly we would better say cross eye—fixed the attention of his audiences. His voice must have been a marvel in carrying power. On one of his voyages to America his ship was traveling in company with another. Both boats one day were becalmed a short distance apart. The request was made that Whitefield preach to both ships at once and Whitefield did so, being heard easily by the audiences on both ships. The report was common in the days of Whitefield's prime that he could be heard a mile, which is not so wonderful if a single call or shout is meant but is not quite credible as referring to a sustained discourse. We have to be on our guard about reports of distances at which the old-time open-air orators could be heard, and also about the size of their audiences. Franklin once made a careful estimate of the power of Whitefield's voice by noticing the

[2] Pp. 89-92.

distance at which he could be heard, measured in Philadelphia blocks. Franklin calculated that twenty-five thousand persons could, under conditions at all favorable, hear and understand Whitefield. The estimate is probably too high.

Whitefield's voice was more than noise. It was perfectly modulated and moved under easy control. The voice naturally and spontaneously adjusted itself to the conditions under which he was speaking. We all remember the oft-quoted remark of David Garrick, an actor of undying fame, as to what he would give if he could pronounce the sound *o* as Whitefield did.

There are some considerations that readily occur to us as adding to the effectiveness of Whitefield's oratory. There was the size of the audiences. Even if we cut the estimates in half, the audiences are still large enough. Again, Whitefield did not have any serious competition from anybody or anything when he appeared to preach in a community. Wherever he went, just about everybody within reach of the notice that he was to preach made haste to be on hand. Again, there were few newspapers. Even if we accept Franklin's estimate that at times Whitefield spoke to twenty-five thousand hearers, we need not suppose that the twenty-five thousand were all newspaper readers. Probably not over a thousand such readers would have been found in any such audience as Franklin measured. The Whitefield sermons had thus all the charm of novelty. Whatever the speaker said was likely to be new to the audience.

What Whitefield said had the appeal of new discovery to those interested in religion. Whitefield, like Wesley, had come to religious power through a deep spiritual crisis. He, like Wesley, had been "seeking the Lord," to use the old expression, by the path of what he called "good works." Whitefield was with Wesley a member of the Holy Club and sought spiritual peace in visiting the jails and other places where he could give relief to the distressed. He had in those days a tendency to asceticism stronger even than that of Wesley, which is saying a good deal. He limited the amount of food which he ate until he began to do serious harm to his body. Strains like this cannot be borne indefinitely. Equilibrium has to be reached or the struggle abandoned. Happily Whitefield attained to peace in his awareness of his relation to God. Some excesses of religious testimony which he recorded in his earlier journals gave offense to many of the English clergy. No doubt Whitefield's statements as to the unworthy state out of which he had climbed and others as to the heights to which he attained were about equally extravagant, but the statements were due to Whitefield's naturally oratorical temperament and to the genuineness of his emotional crises. Through over thirty years of continuous service he had to meet all manner of criticism—criticism as to what we should

call sensationalism, as to irregularity of financial accounts, as to insubordination in his attitude toward
English bishops. Dr. Johnson growled out about
Whitefield as a mountebank and about his "oratory for
the mob," and Horace Walpole peddled some back-
stairs gossip about his unworthily seeking gifts from
the Countess of Huntington and favor from Lord
Dartmouth. The Whitefield mind, however, was
something that Johnson could not be expected to
understand, and any considerable sign of moral uprightness in anybody was enough to loosen Walpole's
poisonous tongue. The evidence is that Whitefield not
only poured into his benevolences, like the Bethesda
Orphanage, all the money he raised by public appeal
but also so much of his own that he kept himself
almost always in distressing impoverishment. As to
sensationalism, anything that makes a sensation is in
the opinion of some men sensational.

People like the Americans of the eighteenth century
cannot be mistaken in their judgment of a religious
leader through a stretch of thirty years. The people
took Whitefield seriously. They were not deceived as
to his genuineness. They realized that in his religious
experience he had seized divine truth and that truth
had seized him. Down under all Whitefield's gifts as
an orator were the deep springs of his own religious
experience which kept welling up in his spoken words.
Scores and hundreds at Whitefield's meetings plied

him with written questions about the ways to God and the duties of genuine religion. The evangelist had the method of asking all in his audiences who sought help from him to send up written questions to the platform. At times the responses were so overwhelmingly numerous as to make impossible any satisfactory handling of them.

Before looking more closely at the religious contribution that Whitefield made to the English colonies, let us mention one general consideration which bore upon that work, namely, the extent of Whitefield's reputation. Carl van Doren, in his life of Benjamin Franklin, has remarked that Whitefield, flying as he did like a shuttle back and forth, especially north and south along the seaboard, was a positive uniting force among the colonies. Whitefield's work was not by any means wholly evangelistic. He was called upon to deliver addresses before all sorts of audiences. He preached at Harvard, at Yale, before colonial legislatures, and upon dedicatory and anniversary occasions. Legislators would put aside their regular tasks in order that he might address them.

These incessant journeys not only furthered a feeling of unity among the colonies, but brought to light a like-mindedness already existing. Whitefield did not vary his preaching to suit different communities. He did not need to. He dealt with themes in which all men have like interests. He came from the England from which most of his hearers had come. He spoke the language of his hearers. Some may regret that Whitefield did not do more to strengthen the ties between the colonies and the homeland. Whitefield did not live to see the inevitable separation of the colonies from England, though he heard the first rumblings of the coming storm. Careful students of his life feel that at the time of his death his sympathies were predominantly American. It is possible that if Whitefield had lived to the Revolution he might have proved a sounder adviser to both England and America than Wesley proved to be, and that for the reason that he knew America better than did Wesley. In the latter half of the eighteenth century Wesley insisted that he knew England better than did anyone else alive—that is, by firsthand contacts. At the same time Whitefield could have said the same about his knowledge of America.

However that may have been, Whitefield was widely known and immensely popular in America. People were ready to listen to him whether they were primarily interested in religion or not.

We are now ready to consider Whitefield's influence on the Calvinists, and for that matter on the Arminian thinking in America. At the time of the Great Awakening under Jonathan Edwards in New England, the religious outlook was Calvinistic. Methodism's official arrival in America was still fully thirty years in the future, so that Methodism did not count in the struggle with Calvinism till long after the period of which I now write. This must be qualified by the remark, however, that in England Wesley was attacking the Calvinistic doctrine of predestination at the time when Whitefield was carrying through his repeated tours in America.

Whitefield was a Calvinist, as was the Countess of Huntington. The Calvinists never came into the Wesleyan societies. They became deeply involved in the controversy with the Arminian Methodists—a battle which became increasingly bitter. Toplady referred to Wesley in savage terms, calling him in one of his less caustic moods an "old fox." Though Wesley and Whitefield had been contemporaries at Oxford, members of the Holy Club together, original Methodists together, the Calvinistic disagreement seriously strained their relationship. In letters to Wesley, Whitefield rebuked him harshly, though Wesley never replied in kind. Indeed, when some of Whitefield's partisans distributed at a service where Wesley was to preach a fierce attack on Wesley which claimed the sanction of Whitefield himself, Wesley went forth and tore up all the copies he could get hold of, remarking that he was only doing what Mr. Whitefield himself would do under like circumstances. The friendship between the two men never broke, though under extreme tension at times. In the personal encounters between them

Wesley shows at considerable advantage over Whitefield, though it is not gracious to say that now. Each
man honored the other till the end of Whitefield's life,
and when that end came John Wesley delivered a
noble funeral eulogy over George Whitefield.

It is not easy to say how thoroughly Whitefield was
a Calvinist. Though he had much to say on the
theme, he does not give the impression, as does Edwards, of having reached his conclusions by profound
and prolonged brooding. He was throughout an evangelist—as Edwards was, for that matter—but he did
not seem to take theological propositions with such
tightness of grip as did Edwards. Again, whether he
knew it or not, Whitefield was always influenced by the
attitude of Lady Huntington. Almost from the first
month of his arrival in America—the reader will recall
that his boat outward bound to Georgia had met that
of Wesley returning to England from Georgia—Whitefield found himself drawn into preaching tours in
America. His fame as a preacher had preceded him.
The bare announcement that he was to preach was
sufficient to call together at the preaching place all the
people who had heard the notice.

Now for a glance at the theological situation. The
Calvinistic tone in American preaching in the eighteenth century was set chiefly by Jonathan Edwards.[3]

[3] The life and character of Edwards have been most admirably portrayed
in the recent biography by Ola Elizabeth Winslow, *Jonathan Edwards,
1703-1758* (Macmillan, 1940).

There were other thinkers, such as Samuel Johnson, of Yale, who wrote and spoke most powerfully on theological themes; but Edwards had the combination of abilities which drew him into the place of leadership. To begin with, he was a metaphysician of the first order. Almost at the outset of his philosophical studies, he drew up a statement of absolute idealism which might easily have been taken as the work of Bishop Berkeley, though we do not know that Edwards ever read a line of Berkeley. It is true that Berkeley spent three years in Rhode Island while Edwards was no farther away than western Massachusetts, but there is nothing to indicate that the two men ever met either in person or by correspondence.

Those beings which have knowledge and consciousness are the Only Proper and Real and Substantial beings inasmuch as the being of other things is Only by these forms hence we see the Gross mistake of those who think material things the most substantial beings and spirits more like a shadow, whereas spirits Only are Properly Substance.[4]

Does not this sound almost like a transcript of some of the most Berkeleian passages of Berkeley?

Edwards had passed through a profound religious experience, which did not indeed bear the marks of crisis as did the conversion of Wesley or that of Whitefield; but to Edwards it was a conversion nevertheless.

[4] "On Being."

So far as conduct was concerned, even a psychologist might have found it difficult to tell from what to what the spiritual change was. For if any youth ever lived a flawless life so far as moral conduct went, that youth was Edwards. He had been reared in a minister's home, where religious themes had been discussed from Jonathan's earliest recollection. There was a fine comradeship between father and son which lasted until death parted the two. Before he was in his teens Edwards was a close observer of natural processes; he wrote an essay on spiders which today shows marks of keenest observational powers. All through his life he was interested in natural science, but his chief themes of contemplation even in youth proved to be first science, after that philosophy—in which he was a student and admirer of John Locke—and finally theology. The conversion seems to have been the crowning of long periods of brooding over the problem of God and of man's relation to God. He describes it as the revelation of new beauty in all that his eyes beheld, a new joy in contemplating the works of God in all realms of creation.

Just about the time that Whitefield reached Georgia to take up the work which Wesley had left, a revival broke out in Northampton where Edwards had begun his twenty-five-year pastorate. The revival was at first local, confined to the reach of Edwards' own ministry. By 1740 it had spread the length of the Connecticut

Valley and thence south. Benjamin Franklin, deist though he was, commented on the change the revival had made in the manners of the people of Philadelphia, though that was after Whitefield had thrown his mighty eloquence into the movement. By the time Whitefield himself got well a-going, the initial impetus given by Edwards had begun to slow down. Whitefield so reinforced the work of Edwards that some students of American religious history go so far as to say that Whitefield saved the Great Awakening.

The point on which I wish to insist is not that Whitefield's preaching complemented that of Edwards, but that it modified it. As a revivalist Edwards worked too intensely to make it possible for the movement as such to last long. Revivals run through well-marked stages. They begin with high power which rushes to a peak and then dies away till some new method or new personal force starts a new interest, or the revival finds a channel for its energies in some institutional agency. There were weaknesses in the Edwards movement.

To begin with, the note of tragedy runs through it all. To be sure, the period itself was tragic. Not all the glorious beauty of the Connecticut Valley could shake from men's minds that life was hard, dreadfully hard, and that death might not be far away. Though the decisive conquest of the Indians had been accomplished, Northampton was still a frontier and any lurking savage in the woods was a peril. Scourges of ter-

rible disease, like smallpox—to inoculation for which
Edwards himself succumbed when he was only fifty
—and mysterious wasting fevers would sweep period-
ically over communities with fearfully fatal results. It
used to be said that something of the power of the
old Roman Church lay in the fact that the priests,
through the power of excommunication, could threaten
men with a hell which seemed to be just around the
corner. The question of hell apart, the people to whom
the Great Awakening ministered knew that death
might be just around the corner.

Moreover, Edwards' preaching was terrorism. Edwards was a thinker of unyielding logic. What logic
called for had to have the right of way. Unsympa-
thetic students have felt that at a time when the Bible
was considered infallible, Edwards put the demands of
reason ahead of the authority of the Scriptures. Probably Edwards would have answered that he had to use
his reason in the interpretation of the Scriptures. Anyhow the logic was remorseless enough. "The soul that
sinneth, it shall die." Admitting this, we cannot see
why Edwards added such horrors of his own to the
death, which after all never could come to an end.
Quite likely Edwards' most awful sermon was "Sinners
in the Hands of an Angry God," in which occurred
the well-known passage:

The God that holds you over the pit of hell, much as one

holds a spider, or some loathsome insect over the fire, abhors you. . . . . You are ten thousand times more abominable in his eyes, than the most hateful venomous serpent is in ours.

Or think of this from "The Future Punishment of the Wicked Unavoidable and Intolerable":

But to help your conception imagine yourself to be cast into a fiery oven, all of a glowing heat, or into the midst of a glowing brick-kiln, or of a great furnace, where your pain would be as much greater than occasioned by accidently touching a coal of fire, as the heat is greater. Imagine also that your body was to lie there for a quarter of an hour, full of fire, as full within and without as a bright coal of fire, all the while full of quick sense; what horror would you feel at the entrance of such a furnace!

So it was to be on and on through eternity.

It would be unpardonable for me to quote such passages if I felt that they would alarm anybody today or would now be taken as anything more than a relic for a theological museum. One strange feature of such preaching—strange considering the logical quality of Edwards' mind—is the miracle involved in a place of perpetual physical torment, requiring as it does the fitting of sinners with a sensory apparatus to make feeling under such conditions possible—a miracle more astonishing than any marvel we ever see in the world around us. What could there have been in the Edwards mind that made it hospitable to any such

horrors as pictured in these sentences? Well, logic
was what was in the Edwards mind. What logic called
for had to be. Edwards was set like a flint against
what we call today "wishful thinking." Yet we cannot
read through the arguments of Edwards without feeling that logic had taken him a willing captive and
that his devotion to logic was a high form of wishful
thinking. Not that Edwards rejoiced in the tortures;
he rejoiced that the logic was to be followed out no
matter what the tortures, and in the rush of the logic
he failed to see that he arrived a considerable distance
beyond where the logic itself carried him.

Samuel Wesley once told his son John that not
everything in life is settled by logic. Wesley was a
greater evangelist than Edwards, partly because he was
not so much of a logician. There is something impersonal about logic, and sooner or later the logician is
almost certain to get the impersonal above the personal.
Nobody ought to seek to pass dogmatically on dogmatic theology unless he is very much of a human
being—and if he is a genuinely human being he is not
likely to pass dogmatically on problems involving
human destiny.

Whitefield served the Great Awakening by being a
human being as well as a devoted evangelist. As a
preacher he did not leave his heaven in a state of unrelieved strain. Edwards is always described as standing erect before his audiences in preaching, stiff and

unyielding, with few or no gestures. There was not much that a listener under stress could do to ease the tension. In my boyhood I remember hearing an old man tell of a tradition about the Edwards preaching which had come down to him at, I think, three generations removed from a member of the congregation who had heard the sermon on "Sinners in the Hands of an Angry God." The tradition was that "sinners" who heard the sermon gripped the benches on which they sat to keep from slipping off into hell. There is not much relief from tension in gripping benches. Edwards could not have been a very attractive or inviting or appealing figure while preaching that sermon. Edwards was not by any means a born orator, and Whitefield was. The born orator has the instinctive ability to adjust himself to the moods of his audience, to lead them along by half yielding to them, easing the pull on their tightened faculties. If he deals with darkness, he turns now and again to light. If he has made drains upon their power of attention, he relieves them by talking commonplace till they recover their breath. We read that Whitefield once portrayed the moral dangers of the unrepentant life by taking advantage of a passing thunderstorm for illustration; but when the storm ceased, he ceased. Upon another occasion he described a shipwreck so vividly to an audience of sailors that they leaped up and began to shout: "Take to the long-boat. Take to the long-boat." This relieved the emotional pressure and left Whitefield free to press home his spiritual appeals in quieter tones. Such was the method of Whitefield, but that sermon of Edwards has no break or let-down; all the terrors are described in a series of carefully numbered points up to ten, the successive stages labeled and placed as carefully as bottles on a shelf.

Again, Whitefield seldom concluded a sermon, whether on an evangelistic theme or other, without giving his hearers something practical on which to take hold. William James used to say that it is morally perilous to allow impulses toward good to pass without some deed expressing the impulse, no matter how insignificant the deed itself may seem. I suppose that Whitefield made his customary appeals for Bethesda at Savannah for the sake of the orphanage, but incidentally he worked with keen oratorical understanding. He seems almost always to have taken a collection: for Bethesda, for the relief of the sufferers from a terrible conflagration in Boston, and once for the repair of damage done by fire to Harvard College.

The peak of the power of the Great Awakening had passed a little after 1740. The revival was itself one of the outstanding events in the history of religion in America, so significant that John Wesley published in England an account of the work of Edwards; but I think the judgment is sound that Whitefield carried forward the revival.

Whitefield could work from the same theological basis as Edwards. Both were theists—Edwards by conviction, Whitefield by that rather spontaneous mood that Dr. Johnson revealed when Boswell spoke to him about Edwards' denial of the freedom of the will: "All theory is against the freedom of the will; all experience for it." This characteristically summary decision of Johnson would probably have satisfied Whitefield, though Whitefield did attempt some arguments, mostly oratorical, in favor of the denial of freedom. Both Edwards and Whitefield believed in devisive, almost violent, conversions; both believed that acceptance by God revealed itself in transformed ethical conduct. Still, under Edwards the religious movement slowed down, and under Whitefield it went ahead. It must not be forgotten, however, that in the revival three hundred out of the six hundred citizens of Northampton were converted under Edwards' guidance.

The religious exactions of Edwards were too stern. Such discipline will do for a season in the spiritual care of souls, but its stiffness makes it break. It is iron and not steel.

Again, Edwards was an aristocrat. He did not know people in the mass. It is recorded that at a meeting in London Whitefield took a collection yielding forty-seven pounds. In that collection there were 7,680 coins. Quite a power of imagination would be required to fit Jonathan Edwards into a scene like that. Altogether apart from the mass of men, Jonathan Edwards expected the individuals not of his own social standing literally to keep their distance. More than ordinary ability is required for an aristocrat to preach the love of God to those whom he considers his inferiors.

Once more, the revival interest dwindled because of difficulties in the Edwards church caused by the pastor's overstrictness and sternness of discipline. In the Northampton church there were two classified grades of members: those who subscribed to the doctrines of the church and supported it by gifts and attendance; and those who gave evidence of something more than the first group—some finer, more saintly quality which entitled them to partake of the sacrament of the Lord's Supper. Edwards himself insisted on saying who possessed the gifts and graces entitling the worshiper to the higher sacramental privileges. The insistence of Edwards upon his authority in what Northampton considered unreasonable requirements started a discussion in the church which ceased only with the dismissal of Edwards in 1750, after a quarter century of service. Tragic as this outcome was, it was inevitable. Logician, aristocrat, disciplinarian—the combination was more than the Northampton church could stand. Indeed, the church was most patient considering that the pastor, as the years went by, demanded the translation of ideals into conduct with a thoroughness to which ordinary human nature could not adjust itself.

Jonathan Edwards was not ashamed of being called a perfectionist. His ideal of perfection was much sounder than John Wesley's. Wesley taught the possibility of attaining moral perfection in one instantaneous spiritual uplift. He escaped a deal of trouble from his questioners by never claiming that he himself had attained the experience, and by limiting the perfection to sinlessness of motive and intention, not extending it to freedom from errors of judgment. This left the whole conception at loose ends. It would be possible to argue that most of the serious evil, at least in the social realm, occurs in wrong practical judgment. I have not been able to find that Edwards preached perfection as an experience attainable in the Wesleyan manner, but he took his idea quite as seriously as Wesley took his. The ideal was to be held always before the life as the constant aim, and he had most lofty interpretations of duty for himself and for everyone else. Wesley was willing to accept testimony from his followers that they had attained perfection. There is nothing to indicate that Edwards would have accepted such a claim from anyone. He would have claimed the authority to be the judge as to the perfection himself.

It was after Edwards had gone to Stockbridge to minister both to the colonists there and to "reservation Indians" that he wrote his famous treatise on the freedom of will. The positive statement of his doctrine has been put forth time and again, sometimes by men who have not seemed to realize that Edwards had formed the argument better than they were putting it, and that he had done so a century and a half before they were born. In brief, Edwards taught that the will chooses but that it can choose only in obedience to the strongest motive, that the motives are the expression of the character of the man himself, and that the man is what he is because God has made him so. This raises forthwith the question whether God himself has anything like freedom as being able to make choices. Edwards could only reply that God could only make such choices as his nature called for, which anyone understanding the Arminian doctrine could accept, but not on Edwards' own understanding. For Edwards was not entitled to believe that God himself could choose in any humanly intelligible manner.

Edwards own attack on the freedom of the will declared that such a choice as the doctrine called for had to be an uncaused cause, unless back of each choice was another choice which caused the first, and another which caused the one which caused the first, and so on indefinitely. The conception of a self with a power, limited but real, to choose between two courses was abhorrent to him. If the self chose one course rather than another, that meant that the self preferred one rather than the other, and preference meant motive determining the choice. Anything else for Edwards meant a cause without a cause. The free-willer declared that God was the cause of the finite self and had dowered it with such independence as to make free choice possible.

It was not on such questions as choice as an uncaused cause that the free-willers, especially in England and including John Wesley, assailed all types of Calvinism, Edwardean included. They took their stand on the moral nature of God. Edwards had an expedient that proposed to save God's character, but it was oversubtle and overingenious. Man has two sets of qualities, the lower and the higher—the lower what men ordinarily call the flesh, and the higher the moral and spiritual. God is the cause of evil, not as positively causing it, but as permitting the withdrawal of his higher gifts to men, leaving the lower qualities soon to run rampant into rebellion. Why a holy God should thus allow the higher qualities to loosen their control did not appear.

In one form or another the Calvinist debate ran on till first Edwards and then Whitefield and then Wesley had passed from the earthly scene. It reached pretty far down into the discussion groups of quite ordinary men, by which I mean those not trained to theological debate. It might have been a deterrent and hindrance to the larger interests of religion if it had not been that the ordinary man is not deeply moved by logic. If he felt powerless to answer Edwards in logical terms, he saw that Whitefield did not lay overmuch stress on logic but moved in the realms of the emotions where the ordinary man lives. Indeed, what prevented the Edwards logic from going too far on the one hand, and what saved much of the logic on the other, was the emotionalism of which Whitefield was such a master. In his earlier days Edwards himself laid stress on the religious value of emotionalism—in fact, himself abounded in a rich and full emotional experience. To that emotionalism his rocklike logic was a contradiction, or perhaps the other way round: the emotionalism set limits to the logic, at least in the minds to which the freedom of the will spoke. However it may be about the emotionalism of Edwards himself, there can be no doubt as to the effect of Whitefield's oratory. It had in it the tingle of life. People knew that Whitefield was the close friend of Wesley, and that Wesley was a free-willer as Whitefield was not, but that both were more absorbed in the transformation of the lives of their fellow men than in abstract theological debate. So to a degree they accepted Whitefield's Calvinism but were swayed by his humanity and his devotion to his fellow men. It came to pass thus that Whitefield was accredited with having helped in the foundation of 150 Congregational churches. It is estimated also that Whitefield's converts were reckoned by terms of thousands.

Whitefield had to meet criticism from two ecclesiastical groups. On the one hand, the Church of England leaders claimed that he was lacking in loyalty to the church in acting so entirely as a free lance. We may perhaps judge the force of this criticism by asking what difference it would have made in Whitefield's work if he had been as subservient to the English bishops as they expected him to be. It would have made a vast difference. If Bishop Butler could say to John Wesley that Methodist assurance in religious testimony was a "very horrid thing, Sir," we can only imagine what the bishops of lesser caliber would have demanded of Whitefield. Whitefield would have got nowhere under the orders of English bishops. Moreover, his independency helped the New England churches to an autonomous self-reliance which aided American Christianity mightily in the eighteenth century. The new country needed both centralized Methodism and independent Congregationalism.

The other criticism was that Whitefield in his work in America was not Methodistic enough. Methodism was not counting, however, as much of a distinctive force in America during Whitefield's days here. Methodists had begun to arrive in America; but the first church was built only four years before Whitefield's death, and the Methodist Episcopal Church was not organized till fourteen years after Whitefield had gone. Whitefield was a prodigious, inspirational character, but not an ecclesiastical administrator. The Countess of Huntington tried to get him to supervise the work of her fifty and more chapels, but he soon dropped supervision and turned again to his long evangelistic pilgrimages.

The early Methodist preachers in America, following the example of Wesley, talked valiantly against Calvinism and did much to rob it of its terrors. Nevertheless, Edwards' teaching had lasting values. The Methodists did preach as if the free will could do about as it pleased, in defiance of God. The truth that God, as knowing all the possible consequences of free choices, could adjust the consequences to further his own plans did not seem to occur to the Methodists. A modified Calvinism held that a free will could freely accept God's plan and march ahead with it, or freely reject it and be dragged along. Edwards did mightily enforce the idea of divine laws. More than that, he profoundly understood the stirrings of religious impulses in the soul and the differences in forms of religious experience. He reveled in the beauties of law. He was almost ecstatic in his contemplation of the glories of the universe as taught by Newton, the beauties of proportion and symmetry in the creation of the world. He could have understood the line of Edna St. Vincent Millay, "Euclid alone hath looked on Beauty bare."

Whitefield, however, was on the side of the more genuine humanity. We know that while the church saves the world, the world at times of religious overstrain saves the church by its commonplace, everyday demands for mental and spiritual wholesomeness. The soul saves the body; but at times when the soul gets too far above the earth, the body saves the soul. Those who are fond of insisting that Whitefield was not a superior intellect forget that it was a profusion of qualities other than the strictly intellectual which helped to keep religion close to human life in eighteenth-century America.

THOMAS PAINE

I AM somewhat embarrassed in announcing the subject of this chapter. The series has to do with English contributions to American thought and action. It is hard to say whether we can give the credit to England for what Paine did or did not do. He was indeed born in England in 1737 and was thirty-eight years old when he came to America; but he was so un-English, not to say anti-English, when he reached America that one is tempted to call him an American from the start. In addition, one shrinks, at least at first, from calling Paine's work in religion a contribution to American religion. He certainly had no intention of lending any aid to Christianity here or anywhere.

Nevertheless, we cannot look at religious movements either in England or America without considering deism, and if we are to consider deism in this country we cannot leave Paine out. While he cannot be considered an original thinker on religious themes, yet he possessed the power of getting his ideas into the minds of the masses to a larger measure than any other man of his time. From the date of the publication of *The Age of Reason* in 1794-95 no writer on deism in America got far without referring to Paine. That was the decisive date in the American attitude toward Paine. True, the references to *The Age of Reason* were most vituperative, but the references were to *The Age of Reason* nevertheless. Practically all the arguments for and against deism after the appearance of Paine's book dealt with the book. While Paine never carried deism to any notable victory, he it was who set the targets at which the defenders of Christianity aimed their bolts. Probably the formal theologians would prefer to deal with some more conventionally correct figure than Paine in discussing deism, but Paine is the figure the professional theologian cannot escape or ignore.

On the philosophical side deism is the most important religious theme of the middle eighteenth century. It is not the most logical philosophy but the most important. In England the deistic writers had been significant enough to call forth rejoinders from minds as powerful as Bishop Butler, of the famous *Analogy,* and Bishop Berkeley, the founder of English idealism. Some attention has been paid to deism in America. Anyone familiar with Jonathan Edwards knows how intolerable the Edwards system must have been with the passing of the years. Perhaps it is too much to say that a reaction was inevitable, but sooner or later there had to be an easing up or a softening of Calvinism. There is plenty of reason to believe that many of the theological descendants of Edwards had let down considerably in their Calvinism and were sympathetic to the deistic writings which were finding their way across the sea from London. I do not mean that these leaders were advocating deism or even accepting it, but they were at least reading it and, presumably, talking about it. Edwards had died in 1758. The storm caused by *The Age of Reason* came nearly forty years later. It would not have been possible for Calvinism to have remained unchanged during four decades, and the change had to be in the direction of dulling the edge and softening the material.

Of Paine it is especially true that we cannot understand his book without knowing something of the man. When we take into account the incredible efficiency of Paine's mature life, to say nothing of its breathtaking romantic episodes, it is strange that we have so little record of his earlier circumstances. Always poor, he began his working life as a corset maker. He had two domestic tragedies, the loss of his first wife by death and of the second by her divorce from him. There is a tradition that in the days when Methodism was coming to power in England Paine imitated the lay preachers by speaking in public to Methodists wherever he could—a tradition which seems to have carried over into America, for there are still casual but persistent claims of discoveries of references to Paine's speaking as a layman to Methodist groups in New Jersey. There is no reason why this should be out of the question. In the earlier years what few references

to religion Paine made were not in the bitter temper
of those of *The Age of Reason.* Benjamin Franklin
met Paine in London in the early seventies and sug-
gested a journey to America. Paine eagerly accepted
the suggestion and arrived in America in early 1775.

From first acquaintance with Paine we see one trait
clearly—his hatred of privilege in any form. The England of his day was honeycombed with privilege, or
rather it was completely graduated into scales of privilege. There was first the King. By the time Paine
sailed for America, George was fighting a life-and-
death battle for the privileges of his crown. There was
the nobility, greedy for money without working for it.
There was the Established Church. More than these,
and altogether apart from legal enactment, there were
gradations, not of rank necessarily, but of social standing, which reached clear down into the relationships
of villagers to one another.

On reaching America, Paine seems to have discovered
at once that this was his field. There is not another
quite so striking instance of a newcomer's at once seiz-
ing opportunity for popular leadership as Paine's experience in America. The air was quivering with resentment against England's rule of the colonies; and though
the anti-English sentiment was not nearly unanimous,
and in fact never came to be, there was an increasingly
heavy majority against England. A leader was needed
to crystallize that majority discontent—to bring it to a

head, or a crisis. Paine's *Common Sense* did that. It required a born pamphleteer, and Paine was that. His straightforward statement of America's case was inevitable, indeed irresistible. One million copies of the pamphlet were circulated in a few weeks, as fast as post horses could carry them through the colonies. The leaders from George Washington down gave Paine credit for the development of the popular sentiment which made the Declaration of Independence possible. More than that, the thirteen *Crisis* papers kept the American spirit alive till independence had been won by force of arms and peace granted by treaty. Paine thought of himself as having won his first battle against privilege.

He began at once on the second. Paine was by nature an inventive genius. He had a passion for drawing plans of bridges and went so far with the model of an iron bridge with a longer span than any other then known that he went to France and England to enlist support for his project. The story of the bridge, interesting enough in itself, has nothing to do with this chapter, and, after a little, had not much to do with Paine's career. For in England Paine saw anew the widespread curse of a privilege from which he supposed he had seen America freed. Edmund Burke was writing his *Reflections on the French Revolution,* when the revolution had not yet run to excess; and Paine replied to the conservatism of Burke so effectively that, though he had left England, he was tried before an English court for libeling the British Constitution, found guilty, and declared an outlaw. Thereafter the British officials were on the watch for Paine. One reason for his long stay in France was that England with her command of the sea would have seized any ship on which Paine was supposed to be sailing, and that would have been the end of his pamphleteering activities. *The Rights of Man,* written in reply to Burke, is probably Paine's ablest work, and few abler have ever appeared in its field.

Expelled from England, Paine was heartily welcomed by revolutionary France, was made a citizen of the Republic, and, admitted to its legislature, he fought against his old foe privilege until quiet times came again. He was a moderate in politics, nearly losing his head because of Robespierre's rage against his not being more radical—loss from which he was spared by the change of French sentiment which cut off Robespierre's own head. As it was, Paine lay more than a year in a foul prison under what was virtually sentence of death, from which he was released by the swing of sentiment and by the incessant labor of James Monroe. During Paine's residence in France, the Federalists had come into control in the United States; and Paine, because of his revolutionary sympathies, was out of favor with the Federalists. Even though Paine was in mortal peril, President Washington did nothing in his behalf.

After being released Paine remained five years longer in Paris. At one time he was in good standing with Napoleon Bonaparte but lost that standing through not approving Bonaparte's proposed invasion of England, taking the ground that even if the invasion were successful, it would not accomplish the change in England that Paine thought desirable. Paine returned to America in the administration of Thomas Jefferson, who was both pleased and embarrassed at his friendship; for by the time of his return *The Age of Reason* had been distributed all over America and had called forth a storm of abuse which has hardly had a parallel in our history. The famous characterization of him was that of Theodore Roosevelt, who called him a "filthy little atheist." This judgment was pronounced in a biography of Gouverneur Morris written by Roosevelt. If one cares to know Morris's opinion of Paine, one has only to dip here and there into the recently published diary of Morris, the unexpurgated edition. The charge that Morris detested the revolutionary views of Paine so heartily that he was anxious to see him guillotined may be extreme, but there can be no doubt about the attitude of the aristocratic Morris toward the man who thought that America was under some debt to France for help given in the revolution which freed the colonies. Paine was not little—five feet, nine inches physically, and intellectually giant enough to shake the social system of three nations. The only filthiness about him was that of poverty, and he was not an atheist at all, but a foe of atheism.

The impression has been commonly spread that the real objection in America to Paine was his lack of religious orthodoxy—that because of his services to the new nation in *Common Sense* and the *Crisis* papers the heresy of Paine was borne with by American political and educational and religious leaders until his irreligion could be endured no longer and those leaders reluctantly repudiated him. This is just about as far from the truth as any judgment of the kind could well be. The American Revolution was not radical but conservative. The colonies were glad for any help they could get against England from France or anywhere else. The religious leaders themselves were tinctured with deism. As has already been said, during the time of the earlier circulation of *The Age of Reason* the leadership of America was that of the upholders of privilege—the privilege which Paine hated. The supporters of privilege hated Paine for hating privilege, and turned against him as soon as they could safely do so. *The Age of Reason* supplied to the upholders of American privilege the best conceivable ground on which to attack Paine. He had fought against privilege from 1778 to 1794 in terms which were difficult to meet. When he could be branded as infidel his enemies had the best weapon against him. Looking back to those stormy times, we may be sure that while there were hosts of sincere people who were sadly distressed at Paine's deism, the furious opposition came not from his religious heresy but from social heresy—the heresy of opposition to social privilege. We have only to look at the Constitution of the United States to see the distrust of the people which actuated the founding fathers. Can anyone imagine that the followers of Alexander Hamilton, for example, who poured out their rage against Paine's teachings about religion were chiefly disturbed about religion? The friendliness of Paine toward French revolutionary doctrines was the chief cause of the fury of the Federalists toward him.

Now we come to one of the most striking facts about *The Age of Reason*. It was not written against religion as such but against *atheism*. Paine was distressed by the avowed atheism of the more radical French leaders. He felt that the blank atheism would prove the death of the French experiment and conceived his task at the moment to be avowed warfare against the course which the French radicals were taking. In two directions Paine was seeking a moderate path: that between atheism and orthodox Christianity, and that between government by all the French people and government by what we should call today the dictatorship of the proletariat. Paine was out-and-out against class rule by any single group in society.

It is time now to state Paine's creed as found on the first two pages of *The Age of Reason:*

The circumstance that has now taken place in France of the total abolition of the whole national order of priesthood, and of everything appertaining to compulsive systems of religion, and compulsive articles of faith . . . . [has] rendered a work of this kind [*The Age of Reason*] exceedingly necessary, lest in the general wreck of superstition, of false systems of government, and false theology, we lose sight of morality, of humanity, and of the theology that is true.

As several of my colleagues, and others of my fellow-citizens of France, have given me the example of making their voluntary and individual profession of faith, I also will make mine; and I do this with all that sincerity and frankness with which the mind of man communicates with itself.

I believe in one God, and no more; and I hope for happiness beyond this life.

I believe in the equality of man; and I believe that religious duties consist in doing justice, loving mercy, and endeavoring to make our fellow creatures happy.

But lest it be supposed that I believe many other things in addition to these, I shall in the progress of this work, declare the things I do not believe, and my reasons for not believing them.

I do not believe in the creed professed by the Jewish Church, by the Roman Church, by the Greek Church, by the Turkish Church, by the Protestant Church nor by any church that I know of. My own mind is my own Church.

All national institutions of churches, whether Jewish, Christian, or Turkish appear to me no other than human inventions, set up to terrify and enslave mankind, and monopolize power and profit.

I do not mean by this declaration to condemn those who believe otherwise; they have the same right to their belief as I have to mine. But it is necessary to the happiness of man that he be mentally faithful to himself. Infidelity does not consist in believing or in disbelieving: it consists in professing to believe what he does not believe.

In a word, Paine professed that he did not believe in any form of supposedly *revealed* religion—Catholic, Jewish, Mohammedan, or Protestant. A more summary method of setting just about all the believers on earth against him in one swift stroke could hardly be imagined, for all the forms of religion he denounced assert belief in some type and degree of divine revelation. Manifestly, Paine was not thinking of consequences harmful to himself when he wrote the first pages of *The Age of Reason,* or any other pages for that matter. The book could never attain the success he hoped for it, yet he was writing sincerely in the hope that he was doing something for the deliverance of mankind from slavery.

I shall not attempt any formal refutation of Paine's arguments. There is no use in sticking spears into dead lions. Enough of the argument should, of course, be given to help us to understand Paine. Much of it belongs so wholly to the times in which it was written that it has little meaning today. Some needs no answering; some answers itself. Some, however, has perennial value, not because of its inherent worth, but because it keeps constantly recurring.

I may be permitted to refer again to the storms of criticism raised against Paine. So much of the smoke of abuse hung over the deistic battlefield that it is hard at times to see what shots on either side were taking effect. To begin with, the temper of debate in those times was ferocious as soon as any vital interests were aroused. President Lowell once referred to some of the debates of the early political leaders at the beginning of the nineteenth century as models, citing a reference in the diary of a political opponent to a speech made by John Marshall—reference which abounded in praise for Marshall. It happened, however, that the diary was that of Thomas Jefferson, and Jefferson's moderation of speech could not be taken as typical of the times. Vituperation, talebearing, slander, epithet hurling, were supposed to be legitimate weapons in any debate, political or religious. Of course, much of this mood persists to this day; but it is now driven under cover, where it runs its poisonous course in whispering campaigns and innuendo. In Paine's day accusations were made in the open, leading to the conclusion as we read them that the times were desperately bad. They were bad enough. And Paine was a favorite target.

Nothing would be gained in retailing here the attacks on Paine. Timothy Dwight, president of Yale during the period of the candidacy of Thomas Jefferson for the presidency, was a violent opponent of Jefferson. Dwight was the grandson of Jonathan Edwards and himself an excellent gentleman and a most serviceable public leader. Without reflecting at all on the sincerity of Dwight we must express a doubt as to whether his feeling against Paine was as much the dislike of a Christian for an anti-Christian as the hatred of a Federalist for a Democrat.

Before we go further we must say that the attacks on *The Age of Reason* were more virulent against the personal character of the author than against the contents of the book. Common understanding was that Paine was a drunkard and that during his discouragement over the failure of the French experiment in republicanism Paine drank heavily. It is difficult, however, to see how Paine could have been a sot and have been so productive an author. As to his being a libertine, there is no proof of that beyond the kind of company he kept in his days of revolutionary agitation. Here we must not forget that a reformer cannot choose his company. In his replies to attacks made upon him Paine was much more restrained than his assailants.

As to the book itself, the first part was written, not while Paine was actually Robespierre's prisoner within jail walls, but while he was under constant police observation in a limited district in Paris. Strange to say, Paine wrote the first part of the book without a Bible at hand. From this angle the work is a marvel, though indeed a stunt-marvel. He must have been a most careful reader of the Bible and have possessed a most remarkable memory.

To a reader of today *The Age of Reason* is in parts disgusting. Its attacks on the story of the virgin birth will hardly bear repeating, not so much because of blasphemy as because of their sheer repulsiveness. The attacks were not blasphemous in Paine's own eyes. He did not accept the Bible as in any manner or degree a divine revelation. With his repudiation of revelation the attacks on the Scriptures did not seem to him blasphemous, but the Scriptures themselves seemed blasphemous because of what he thought of as attributing falsity to God. In reading over some of the worst passages of *The Age of Reason* we must not forget that what Paine wrote was what many of his followers believed from their own reading of the Scriptures.

It has been to the glory of Christianity that it has dared take the risks of publishing its sacred writings. The church leaders who protested against the publication spoke out of intelligible fear as to what might happen if the Scriptures fell into the hands of readers without interpreters. When the church leaders first began to allow the laity to read the Bible, they did so with the book chained to a reading desk in the cathedral, partly no doubt to avoid losing the book, but partly to see who was reading and how much he was reading. The translation of the Scriptures into the vernacular of the various peoples was a fine act of confidence in the Scriptures, and in the people as well, for there is no denying that the impression produced by the reading of some passages of the Bible, taken by themselves, must have been perplexing and confusing to some minds. I think this faith in the Scriptures themselves is a tribute to those who put the sacred writings before the people.

Now with all allowance for Paine's sincerity and his aim at delivering believers from what he conceived to be superstition, he must be paid the dubious compliment of having presented the Scriptures in the worst possible light. That task he did once for all.

Paine was not a profound mind. He played up the contradictions in the Scriptures which anybody could have seen who might have taken the pains to look for them, or who was sharp-eyed enough to notice them. Quite likely the ordinary reader who did notice the contradictions just assumed that there was some explanation and let it go at that, finding parts free from contradiction which did minister to his needs. Paine made much sport over the notion that if Moses wrote the Pentateuch he must have written the account of his own death. He insisted that Moses could not have written the first five books of the Old Testament and made much of the deliberate deception in attributing Scripture passages to men who could not have written them. He arrayed lists of mistaken dates, and genealogies that could not be reconciled with one another.

He had much to say about the amount of testimony that would be required to prove what we would ordinarily call a miracle. It was in such paths that his criticism moved, page after page and chapter after chapter.

His treatment was wooden and mechanical. There is hardly any trace of what one would call either artistic or spiritual discernment. The sublimest passages of Job meant nothing; the Psalms meant nothing; the prayers of course meant nothing; and religious insight was out of the question. The reader of today can read through *The Age of Reason* and marvel at the sharp-eyed keenness of the writer in detecting what eyesight could see, and marvel even more at the utter lack of insight which could, with such literal familiarity with the Bible, find just nothing at all of spiritual suggestiveness, not to say spiritual illumination. Here again it must be admitted that there were thousands of other readers who, if they read the Scriptures at all, followed the literal Paine method and got nothing from them except the contradictions and what seemed to them the most palpable mistakes. The letter was aided by Paine in its work of killing, and the spirit that giveth life got no chance. It must be admitted that too much Christian rejoiner to Paine moved on the plane of Paine's own choosing—the plane of the literal in which the literal could not be conquered.

Not only is there no notable spiritual insight in

Paine; there is no marked historical sense either. It is strange that one who believed in progress put everything on the same plane in the study of the Scriptures. The defender of the Scriptures, according to Paine, made all parts of the Holy Bible alike divine, which meant that he himself thought of them as alike false. There is considerable debate among historical and social students as to when men began to think in terms of progress; but there is no doubt there has always been some progress in the career of mankind, whether men have thought it or not. Men have always tried to get better ways of controlling material forces, of making better tools. It may be that the purpose has been merely to make the tasks and burdens of life easier, without larger aims; but even the struggle for a more comfortable life has helped on toward progressive thinking. Paine does not have much place for forward movement in the religious career of the race, or at least that part of it that has believed in the Bible. True, he does occasionally utter a shrewd observation which does not fit into this static conception. For example, he encounters the defense of the Scriptures that affirms that in the explanation of miracles and other such phenomena, good men have resorted to pious fraud. The trouble with pious fraud, says Paine, is that "it begets a calamitous necessity of going on." Such movement is about all that Paine sees in the Bible, an evil movement downhill with increasing and disastrous speed.

I do not apologize for repeated mention of some of the Paine discussion which now sounds like far-off things and battles long ago. The Paine discussion is far-off to those who take the modern view of the scriptural revelation, but there are multitudes of Christians still who look upon all of the Bible as upon the same plane, not as all alike evil as did Paine, but as all alike good. Study of human nature does not bear out the dictum that the human mind cannot long endure within itself definite contradictions. In the social movement contradictions of ideas come at last to open battle, but not always so in the minds of individuals. The contradiction between the moral ideals of the Old Testament and those of the New have found lodgment in the minds of multitudes of good men without any intellectual or moral explosion whatever. Paine did have a realization of contradictions which carried him into revolt against the Scriptures, and he sought to provoke like explosion in other minds.

There were those who seriously sought to meet Paine on his own grounds. The most noteworthy of these was Bishop Watson of Llandaff. A distinguished historian of the Church of England during the eighteenth century, Dr. J. H. Overton, has told us that in many characteristics Watson was himself not an ideal bishop. The most serious charge is that Watson cared too much for official preferment, but that was a common enough failing in all official circles in the eighteenth century, including the ecclesiastical. Watson wrote a little book called *An Apology for the Bible,* the title which called forth the famous comment of George III that he had not known that the Bible needed an apology, which remark may have indicated George's lack of familiarity with the terminology of theological discussion. In opening Watson's *Apology* one is aware at once of an altogether different atmosphere from that of Paine's *Age of Reason.* To begin with, there is a complete absence of vituperation, which is the difference also between Watson's reply to Paine and that of almost all the other writers against him. I must record again the amazement one feels at the bitterness of those old-time debates. John Wesley is given credit by almost all students of the time for complete freedom from such ferocity of temper; but even he, in his younger days, wrote an attack upon Berkeley's idealism as "deceitful." What in the intellectual universe could ever have prompted the use of the charge of deceit against the advocacy of idealism is difficult to see. Now *The Age of Reason* is a book that aroused wrath aplenty and in its day could be expected to call forth volleys of epithets. The epithets are not to be found in the *Apology.* Considering that it was written in so stormy a time, against a book which was avowedly provocative, by a bishop of that Established Church which Paine so thoroughly detested, the *Apology* is a moral marvel.

Even Paine himself admitted the magnanimity of the Bishop.

The *Apology* is probably on the argumentative side also the most effective reply to Paine. Certainly it reached an enormous circulation for the times in America. We shall have reason in a moment to see that Paine's argument finally lost its force not primarily because of any formal replies; but Watson wrote the most cogent of such replies.

The Bishop had to move within admitted limitations. I may have spoken as if Paine's putting all parts of the Bible on the same plane was his own conception, but it was more than that—a conception common at the time, as indeed it is to this day where the theory of verbal infallibility is held. This was a heavy handicap at the outset. Even with such a disadvantage Watson did wonderfully well. He showed that too much had been made of the contradictions, and showed some of the most difficult mysteries of the Scriptures as reasonable enough in their setting. The following excerpts are quoted from *An Apology for the Bible:*

Sɪʀ,—I have lately met with a book of yours, entitled, "Tʜᴇ Aɢᴇ ᴏғ Rᴇᴀsᴏɴ, Part the Second, being an investigation of true and of fabulous theology;" and I think it not inconsistent with my station, and the duty I owe to society, to trouble you and the world with some observations on so extraordinary a performance. Extraordinary I esteem it; not from any novelty in the objections which you have produced against revealed reli-

gion, (for I find little or no novelty in them,) but from the zeal with which you labor to disseminate your opinions, and from the confidence with which you esteem them true. You perceive, by this, that I give you credit for your sincerity, how much soever I question your wisdom, in writing in such a manner on such a subject; and I have no reluctance in acknowledging that you possess a considerable share of energy of language, and acuteness of investigation; though I must be allowed to lament that these talents have not been applied in a manner more useful to human kind, and more creditable to yourself.
. . . .

In this part, your ideas seem to me to be confused: I do not say that you, designedly, jumble together mathematical science and historical evidence; the knowledge acquired by demonstration, and the probability derived from testimony. You know but of one ancient book, that authoritatively challenges universal consent and belief, and that is Euclid's Elements. If I were disposed to make frivolous objections, I should say, that even Euclid's Elements had not met with universal consent; that there had been men, both in ancient and modern times, who had questioned the intuitive evidence of some of his axioms, and denied the justness of some of his demonstrations; but admitting the truth, I do not see the pertinency of your observation. You are attempting to subvert the authenticity of the Bible, and you tell us that Euclid's Elements are certainly true. What then? Does it follow that the Bible is certainly false? The most illiterate scrivener in the kingdom does not want to be informed, that the examples in his Wingate's Arithmetic are proved by a different kind of reasoning from that by which he persuades himself to believe, that there was such a person as Henry VIII., or that there is such a city as Paris. . . . .

Your argument stands thus—if it be found that the books

ascribed to Moses, Joshua, and Samuel, were not written by Moses, Joshua and Samuel, every part of the authority and authenticity of these books is gone at once. I presume to think otherwise. The genuineness of these books (in the judgment of those who say that they were written by these authors) will certainly be gone; but their authenticity may remain: they may still contain a true account of real transactions, though the names of the writers of them should be found to be different from what they are generally esteemed to be. . . . .

What if I should admit, that Samuel, or Ezra, or some other learned Jew, composed these books, from public records, many years after the death of Moses? Will it follow, that there was no truth in them? . . . . every fact recorded in them may be true, whenever, or by whomsoever they were written. . . . .

You think "that law in Deuteronomy inhuman and brutal, which authorized parents, the father and mother, to bring their own children to have them stoned to death for what it is pleased to call stubbornness." You are aware, I suppose, that paternal power amongst the Romans, the Gauls, the Persians, and other nations, was of the most arbitrary kind; that it extended to the taking away the life of the child. I do not know whether the Israelites in the time of Moses exercised this paternal power: it was not a custom adopted by all nations, but it was by many; and in the infancy of society, before individual families had coalesced into communities, it was probably very general. Now, Moses, by this law, which you esteem brutal and inhuman, hindered such an extravagant power from being either introduced or exercised among the Israelites. This law is so far from countenancing the arbitrary power of a father over the life of his child, that it takes from him the power of accusing the child before a magistrate: the father and the mother of the child must agree in bringing the child to judgment; and it is not by their united will that the child was to be condemned to death: the elders of the city were to judge whether the accusation was true; and the accusation was to be not merely, as you insinuate, that the child was stubborn, but that he was, "stubborn and rebellious, a glutton and a drunkard." Considered in this light, you must allow the law to have been a humane restriction of a power improper to be lodged with any parent. . . . .

My philosophy teaches me to doubt of many things; but it does not teach me to reject every testimony which is opposite to my experience: had I been born in Shetland, I could, on proper testimony, have believed in the existence of the Lincolnshire ox, or of the largest dray horse in London; though the oxen and horses in Shetland had not been bigger than mastiffs. . . . .

If several honest men should agree in saying that they saw the King of France beheaded, though they should disagree as to the figure of the guillotine or the size of his executioner, as to the king's hands being bound or loose, as to his being composed or agitated in ascending the scaffold, yet every court of justice in the world would think that such difference respecting the circumstances of the fact, did not invalidate the evidence respecting the fact itself. When you speak of the whole of a story, you cannot mean every particular circumstance connected with the story, but not essential to it; you must mean the pith and marrow of the story; for it would be impossible to establish the truth of any fact, (of Admirals Byng or Keppel, for example, having neglected or not neglected their duty,) if a disagreement in the evidence of witnesses, in minute points, should be considered as annihilating the weight of their evidence in points of importance. . . . .

Four *unconnected* individuals have each written memoirs of the life of Jesus; from whatever source they derived their

materials, it is evident that they agree in a great many particulars of the last importance; such as the purity of his manners; the sanctity of his doctrines; the multitude and publicity of his miracles; the persecuting spirit of his enemies; the manner of his death; and the certainty of his resurrection; and whilst they agree in these great points, their disagreement in points of little consequence is rather a confirmation of the truth, than an indication of the falsehood of their several accounts. Had they agreed in nothing, their testimony ought to have been rejected as a legendary tale; had they agreed in everything, it might have been suspected that, instead of unconnected individuals, they were a set of impostors. The manner in which the evangelists have recorded the particulars of the life of Jesus, is wholly conformable to what we experience in other biographers, and claims our highest assent to its truth, notwithstanding the force of your incontrovertible proposition.
. . . .

Great and laudable pains have been taken, by many learned men, to harmonize the several accounts given us by the evangelists of the resurrection. It does not seem to me to be a matter of any great consequence to Christianity, whether the accounts can in every minute particular be harmonized or not, since there is no such discordance in them as to render the fact of the resurrection doubtful to any impartial mind. If any man in a court of justice should give positive evidence of a fact, and three others should afterwards be examined, and all of them should confirm the evidence of the first, as to the fact, but should apparently differ from him and from each other, by being more or less particular in their accounts of the circumstances attending the fact, ought we to doubt of the fact, because we could not harmonize the evidence respecting the circumstances relating to it? [1]

[1] From Letters I, II, III, VII.

Watson showed also the unreasonable and, indeed, irrational nature of the notion that the Bible was the product of fraud. Paine's case would have been much stronger if he could have talked of error rather than of fraud; but Paine could not have done that and have been Paine, with Paine's experience of, and resentment against, the injustices, perpetuated by privilege. Paine had to be a rebel, an agitator, and not an historian.

The truth seems clear at this distance that Paine was under the influence of what might be called the bad men theory of history. There was a period not so long ago when historians made everything significant in the career of the world depend upon the activities of great men. Then came a reaction with the stress laid upon the play and interplay of almost impersonal forces. The position today is probably sounder which recognizes worth in both positions. There are vast forces, partly economic, partly social, partly anything else, which determine the conditions under which men live in this world, these forces expressed and controlled by powerful leaders. Now along with all this, freedom seekers of the Paine type hold to what might be called the bad men theory of history—to the theory that all the institutions of society are creations of men who use them for their own exploitative purposes, that states are tools in the hands of oppressors, that religious organizations are instruments of priests who use pretended supernatural knowledge to make slaves of believers. Students much keener and profounder than ever Paine was today use substantially the same exposition in protest against what they call the bonds and bands which keep men from their highest liberty.

There is enough truth in this interpretation of social processes to put us all on our guard against the capture of institutions by selfish men or groups, but such interpretation is not by any means the last word. One weakness of Paine's treatment is that he never seemed to see the historic necessity of the institutions of society which he denounced. If monarchy was abolished somebody had to do the work which kings had done. To this, of course, Paine's answer was instantaneously forthcoming: the people themselves could do the work.

It is a pleasure to note that in those terrible days of the French Revolution when the populace were determined to put King Louis to death Paine pled for the saving of the King's life to the very last, imperiling his own safety by the urgent and uncompromising protests against carrying the King to the guillotine. It was this insistence that all but brought Paine himself to the guillotine.

Now Paine put kings and ecclesiastic rulers together as the creators and preservers of privilege. He believed that the Scriptures were a deliberate fabrication to support the kings and the ecclesiastics. Here again it is strange that Paine was so one-sided. The denunciations of kings and priests in the Scriptures seem too

obvious to be missed. Indeed, when we take note at all
of the emphasis with which even the Old Testament
passed judgment on kings who exploited the people,
with which the prophets denounced unjust judges, with
which the importance of the ordinary individual was
implied if not openly set on high, our amazement increased. The failure to see that historic institutions
were not ingeniously contrived instruments of exploitation but that they were created to meet inevitable
human needs, even though they had at times been
seized by selfish men for selfish purposes, vitiates much
of what Paine said. Moreover, Paine's insistence upon
the adequacy of the people themselves to wipe out all
institutional instruments of privilege is little consistent
with what he has to say about the agelong deception of
the people. If ecclesiastics by deliberate planning had
been able to deceive the people through all the ages of
history, if so small a number could enslave so large a
mass, the people must have been a weak and stupid lot.
The fact that kingdoms and law courts and ecclesiastical systems served the people, no matter how imper-
fectly, never made adequate impression on the mind of
Paine. He simply would not see that great social institutions could not on a sudden be wiped out, and that
social progress could not be real, unless a newer institution served men better than the old had done.

Returning now to Paine's detailed criticism of the
Old Testament, we must recognize that neither Paine

nor Watson could have dealt satisfactorily with the faults of the Old Testament, simply because Biblical students did not have the apparatus of linguistic, literary, anthropological, archaeological knowledge which they now possess—knowledge it has taken a century to acquire. As for declarations that Moses did not write the first five books of the Bible, that Genesis is patchwork, that the various Biblical books were for centuries attributed to authors who did not write them, that narratives of events show signs of motive, and scores of other such items, modern study has no difficulty at all. That study is much more radical than Paine ever dreamed of being, so far as mere literary detail is concerned, though not by any means radical with the destructive temper of Paine. Indeed, one of the most useful contributions to Biblical understanding in the history of the church has been through modern scientific scrutiny of the Scriptural documents. That this scientific study has its own faults through unsound assumptions and extremes of method and eccentricities of individual scholars there can be no doubt; but there can be no doubt either that the modern study of the Scriptures willingly concedes to Paine, and to others far abler than Paine, all that was true in what he said and then puts it in its place as having slight relevance for Paine's skeptical conclusions.

While we are speaking of scientific research, we have

to remember that, though Paine holds firmly to the belief that nature is the true and adequate revelation of God and that true religion is the contemplation of nature, revelation taken by itself has its mysteries and perplexities. The vast extent of nature, its cruelties, its meaninglessness when taken by itself, are a sterner problem than Paine ever set himself to meditate upon. It is, quantitatively speaking, more of a problem now than it was in 1794, but it was heavy enough and dark enough then. It is probably to Paine's credit that he was so busy trying to help the peoples of the nations on to liberty that he did not pay much attention to distresses that came, as one might say, in the course of nature. He did not think of the woes which crowded so tumultuously into his life as coming so much from God as from his fellow men, and he had faith in men in the mass. With individual men, even the greatest in his day, ranging down from George Washington to Napoleon Bonaparte, he had trouble enough. It drove him nearly to distraction when any one group, particularly the Jacobin, sought to rule the whole in France. He was for all the people.

In some respects Paine anticipated the enlargement of the conception of God. He was most caustic in his assaults on the Biblical authors and the ecclesiastical officials for teaching the doctrine of an arbitrary God, especially one given to cruelty and the enslavement of men. All this pointed to the need of a God who is responsible in the use of power, though Paine did not definitely expound such a doctrine. One of the moral achievements of the past half century has been the increased stress upon the necessity of holding power and responsibility together. One cannot well see how the God of the deist could be regarded as discharging his obligations with a theology that would keep him so far at a distance from the actual ongoings of the world as does deism. No matter what one's opinion about the Biblical teachings, one would think that the world needed a closer relation to God than deism supplies. Still, John Dos Passos in his book on Thomas Paine in the "Living Thoughts Series" declares that most of the presidents of the United States have been deists.

What besides Watson did limit the spread of deism in the early nineteenth century, at which time it appears to have reached its widest influence? Partly the closely reasoned, eloquently presented dogmatic theology of the powerful Timothy Dwight. Probably, also, a remark by Nathan Bangs in his *History of Methodism in the United States* gives us a valuable hint. Bangs was a foremost Methodist leader in his day and understood religious movements as well as any observer of his time. Bangs commends highly the work of Paine as a political writer and dismisses his theology as of no great consequence. The preachers who carried American civilization out to the West acted practically out of the same feeling. They were republican, and their republicanism was largely of the Paine stamp, but they were not deists. So we have the interesting fact that the conservative attempt to stop Paine's republicanism by branding him as a deist and as what was called an infidel did not work. The pioneers found a way to reject deism and to hold fast to Biblical religion. Looked at today, Paine's theology, if we can ignore its roughness and lack of delicacy, was not so much false as inadequate. It fell short, but its influence is not dead yet by any means.

The fury of the attacks by the more privileged groups on Paine's theology has for more than a century led thousands of radically inclined Americans to assume that *The Age of Reason* has been condemned for the same reason as his social views, namely, its intense passion for liberty. This has given added popularity to *The Age of Reason* and still continues its circulation. Within a month of this writing I have bought at a newsstand, for the price of fifteen cents, a paper-covered copy of *The Age of Reason*.

GEORGE BERKELEY

NEARLY all the men whom I have been discussing could be called utopian. Oglethorpe certainly was, and Wesley was in his Georgia adventure. Whitefield was not clearly so; but Paine, in his dream of establishing a republic wherever he went, was manifestly utopian.

Of all in the list George Berkeley was the most notable for idealistic dreams which he found it impossible to put into practice. He was an Irish clergyman, born in 1685, one of the most original and forceful thinkers the eighteenth century produced. A scholar and divine of high order, he early became convinced that society was in grave peril if not educated by methods and systems in which religion had the chief place. He believed also that westward the course of empire takes its way, and that the western empire offered the most promising field for the training of men in religion and philosophy. He determined upon Bermuda as the center of his effort and planned a noble university there for the education of Americans, especially Indians, youths taken captive in the wars. According to Jonathan Swift, Berkeley was of notable persuasive power; and persuasive he must have been, for he prevailed upon Sir Robert Walpole, then Prime Minister, to promise him a grant of twenty thousand pounds for the Bermuda enterprise, though Sir Robert characteristically never seems to have taken the promise seriously. Berkeley took it seriously enough, for he sailed to America, arriving in 1729 on the expectation that parliamentary aid would be forthcoming. He put his own resources into the enterprise, even sailing to America on a ship which he himself hired. He landed at Rhode Island and waited there three years for Walpole's fulfillment of his promise. Walpole finally reported to a friend of Berkeley that as a statesman he could assure Berkeley that the twenty thousand pounds would be forthcoming, but that as a friend he would say that Berkeley would get nothing and ought to return at once to England. So vanished the dream. The dreamer never saw Bermuda. It seems that Berkeley did have some money left after his scheme failed and turned it over to Oglethorpe for work in Georgia. The time spent in Rhode Island was not lost, if we look at the higher values, for it was there that Berkeley wrote *Alciphron,* considered by many his noblest philosophical work.

Berkeley's real contribution to America and to the world, however, was not the Bermuda scheme but his system of idealism. His work in this realm stands alone in thoroughness and cogency. Just at present it appears to be coming into fresh recognition, but it is worthy of consideration at any time for its own value

—a value which possesses the timeless quality of the utterance of the true genius.

In attempting a study of Berkeley I wish to look at him from a point of view somewhat removed from that of scrutiny directed wholly to Berkeley himself. I wish to think of his idealism as interpreted by, modified by, and contrasted with the idealism of the late Borden Parker Bowne, the American who most resembles Berkeley, though Bowne never appears to be a follower of Berkeley. I do this, for one reason, because both Berkeley and Bowne were thoroughgoing evangelicals, though Berkeley is not to be considered a product of the evangelical movement in the more restricted meaning, for Berkeley was gone before that movement came to the crest of its strength in England. Berkeley was, however, essentially evangelical, a Christian of unmistakable devotion, a veritable saint, in marked contrast to the merely formal ecclesiastics of whom there were so many in his time. Bowne was a product of Methodism, and his evangelical training did much to influence his philosophy.

There is another reason, a personal one, for my approaching Berkeley with Bowne in mind. For the last sixteen years of Bowne's life I was closely connected with him as a pupil and friend. I know what was on his mind, especially during the closing years. He was occupied with Berkeleianism. Arrangements were in progress for his delivery of a course of lectures in an important European university, and the lectures were to deal with Berkeley. Bowne died before the arrangements were completed, indeed before he had written the lectures. The trend of his thinking, however, was clear enough from his conversational and classroom discussions.

To understand Berkeley, we must begin with Locke. For him the mind was a *tabula rasa,* or a sheet of white paper on which the outside world prints a report of itself, the *tabula rasa* being passive. In a discussion like mine, altogether introductory to Berkeley, we need not linger on Locke's discussion of primary and secondary qualities; it is enough to say that Berkeley took up Locke's idea from the statement that the mind passively receives the impressions made upon it and started from there. He insisted that in such case anything that could make on the mind impressions similar to those made by the external world would report an outside world. For illustration we might think of the material world in the terms of the modern physicist, who teaches that matter is energy and energy matter and maintains that the external world is not at all composed of lumps of inert stuff. Matter has been done away, or reasoned away, and energy acting upon our organs of sense has taken its place. Berkeley would have found in our current physics confirmation of his theory that inert and passive matter could not make any report of itself. Matter as popularly conceived could not make itself known. Only force or forces could do that. Today materialism of the old schools—the atomistic scheme of indivisible lumps—is dead, with physics as one of the executioners.

Berkeley, however, went farther than this. Not only could matter as such, of the old inert variety, not report itself, it could not even exist. With Berkeley, to exist is to be perceived. The only existence things have is in being perceived. The forces which act upon mind would not themselves act upon mind unless they were in mind as being perceived. It was here that Berkeley encountered criticism like that of Dr. Johnson, who answered Berkeley by striking at a stone with a walking stick. Berkeley did not mean when he said that nothing could be external to mind that nothing could be external to his individual mind. He made the mind of God all-embracing and meant by that to include the ever-working divine will. The stone which resisted Dr. Johnson's walking stick existed as a manifestation of the power of God, which was quite equal to the task of making an unyielding report of itself to Johnson's eyes and through Johnson's walking stick to Johnson's feeling. Much of the criticism of Berkeley warranted Pope's line that coxcombs answer Berkeley with a grin.

Bowne felt that Berkeley had rendered immense service in demolishing materialism. He felt that there was no answering Berkeley's insistence that matter

could not exist except as the creation of mind and that
since it was the expression of mind it could not continue to exist if mind were withdrawn. He felt, too,
that idealism was the one valid argument for theism,
that all the other arguments—ontological, theological,
cosmological, whatever one might call them—were
merely confirmatory.

Berkeley's thought, however, in Bowne's earlier
judgment, was less satisfactory than the German trend
in philosophy which began with Kant.

It will be recalled that Berkeley laid himself open to
the skepticism of Hume by not making enough of the
activity of the self. Nobody can read the *Commonplace Book* by Berkeley without seeing that Berkeley
does recognize the activity of the self, but he does not
bring that activity out into an important enough place:
it is not nearly central enough. The self is allowed to
be too passive. Berkeley said that if there were no
sense impressions there would be no self, or at least no
consciousness of self. Here Hume stepped in—Hume,
by the way, had deep regard for Berkeley, though
there is nothing to indicate that Berkeley knew anything of Hume—and pointed out that in Berkeley's
own system the impressions revealing the self were in
the same plight as the impressions revealing the outside
world. Keep up the impressions which appear to reveal the self and the self remains; let the impressions
cease and there is no self. I repeat that Berkeley left

himself open to this attack. He recognized the self-activity of the self, to speak in cumbersome fashion; but he too often spoke of the self as a bundle of impressions. English philosophy followed the lead given by Hume and became associationistic, which to a greater or less extent it remains today. Thomas Hill Green showed conclusively enough that Locke, Berkeley, and Hume assumed the self, indeed could not make their theories work without it.

The more fruitful development came from Germany. Kant said that Hume awoke him from his "dogmatic slumber." Once awake he established the reality and agency of the self on new and firm foundations. He argued that the self reads off the reports of the world by its own activity. Even if the world reports itself on a *tabula rasa,* an active mind has to read the message. Time and space are forms of the mind's activity, spectacles through which we view the world. Forthwith the question arose as to what is out there if the spectacles are off; and this led to the Kantian doctrine of a *Ding-an-sich* (thing-in-itself), which we cannot know because we cannot see without the spectacles; and here we are in skepticism again, though of a higher form than that of Hume, who smuggled the self into his system while denying its substantial reality. Two small boys were once discussing together the question as to what the deep blue sky is. One said, "It's nothing. There just ain't anything up there." "Yes, I know," replied the other, "but what is it that ain't up there?" Much philosophy has been equally successful in denying the reality of the self in language that assumes its existence.

Bowne followed the lead of Kant to Hegel, who insisted as positively as Berkeley that things must come within thought or go out of existence; and Bowne became what he at first called an objective idealist. For him the active self reads off the messages, sees the pictures, feels the forces of an outside world—an outside world which is the expression of the divine mind but of nothing outside of all mind. The universe consists, then, of the world-ground, which is the supreme self, and of other finite selves in a common objective system where they can come into touch with one another. The present-day theory of matter as energy Bowne accepted as harmonious to his scheme, with the understanding that the energies are those of the divine mind and will.

This objective reference is essential in Bowne's theory. He always insisted so strenuously upon the reality of an outside-ourselves world that it is a mystery how he could ever have been misunderstood here. His question was as to the nature of the "outside." He believed that reality could be only as it could act—that being and acting were synonymous. The essential was as to what the activity was. In making it that of a Self—spelled with a capital—Bowne conceived it as so objective that in many of its activities the Self might have slight reference to finite selves as we know them. I am a self and exist for myself, but in the divine mind I may be fitted into a plan which has no special, certainly no exclusive, reference to myself. This is clearly possible as concerns my physical existence. My body is composed of elements which I do not fully know and whose purpose I do not understand, activities of which the significance may be small for me but large for the universe as a whole. To use Bowne's oft-repeated words, there may be phases of our lives which, so far as those lives themselves are concerned, are not any finite person's affair. This ought to be objective enough. It was annoying to Bowne, insisting as he did upon the objective, to have to repeat that a "blizzard is not merely a tumult in a man's consciousness." He was especially amused and irritated to find that Christian Scientists here and there were using his idealism to prove that the evil forces of human experience are nonexistent. On the one hand, Bowne insisted that the physical universe is so indifferent that we can use it as we please, within the limits of our power—we can use it practically without any question as to whether it was designed for our use or not. And, on the other hand, he held that we are to look upon it as the stage and setting for divine forces.

I have said that Bowne considered idealism the best basis for theism. He did, but he held that the idealist argument does not strictly get us any farther than the belief in mind as back of the universe without telling us the moral nature of the mind. Here he appears to differ from Berkeley, for Berkeley contended that we infer that a worthy God exists by reasoning similar to that by which we infer that a man exists, namely, by argument from what God does. Bowne pronounced this altogether too easy. Any theistic argument, to be self-sufficient, not merely must reach a mind, but must enlighten us as to the nature and quality of the divine mind. Berkeley teaches that formal theistic argument can establish the nature of God and that the nature thus reached is the same as that proclaimed by revelation, such as that on which Christianity builds. Bowne held that this is beyond the grasp of metaphysical reasoning. There will be opportunity to say later that there is material in Berkeley which lends itself to a method similar to that demanded by Bowne, but we are talking now not of what can be found in Berkeley if we look for it but of where his main emphasis is placed. Berkeley was a child of the eighteenth century, with its atmosphere of the glorification of reason —a glorification so complete that at times it made no room for anything resembling ventures of faith at all. Bowne was as close and severe a reasoner as Berkeley. Perhaps for that very reason he knew where reason had to stop.

It is strange what contradictions or paradoxes we encounter when we deal with theorists who try to fit their schemes into the world of things. If a man is to be a leader of socialists, for example, he must often be an uncompromising individualist, as ruthless as any dictator in pushing his own plans into effect. Conversely, if an individualist would come to largest life in himself, he must steep himself in the currents of society. So in the field before us, a thinker cannot well be an idealist without first following realism to its last attainable outpost; and he cannot be secure in his idealism until he understands the limitations of reason. In attempting any comparison of Bowne and Berkeley we must always keep it within our range of vision that Bowne had the advantage of familiarity with the course of philosophy for a century and a half after Berkeley's death. Berkeley died before Kant had become wide-awake from "dogmatic slumber," but Bowne had the advantage of seeing how the associationism following Hume had worked out in England and how Kant's principles had called forth the philosophies of Fichte and Hegel. Strict reasoner though he was, he became convinced that reason was not the exploratory agent in the world's experience. He insisted that the decisive philosophic battles had to be fought out in the realm of assumptions.

Bowne held that we have no right to stick fast to beliefs in spite of positive disproof; but he also held that after we have reached the limits of logical proof we have the right to go beyond proof, assuming whatever conceptions we need for the attainment of full life. His view is not to be identified with the later and present-day pragmatism but with the assumptions of the practical reason as taught by Kant. Readers will remember that after Kant had gone as far as he could with *The Critique of Pure Reason,* he called in the practical reason to give us a basis for belief in God, freedom, and immortality. By the way, Bowne believed that if Kant had only cleared up the contradictions in his formal philosophy there would not have been much left for any succeeding metaphysics to do.

Just a word about freedom. Berkeley seemed to take human freedom for granted, though with some remarks, especially in the *Commonplace Book,* which seem to imply that a force back of the will itself is acting upon the will. Nevertheless, Berkeley was a defender of freedom. While Bowne believed that freedom cannot be logically proved, he was sure nothing could be proved except on the assumption of freedom; for freedom implies the power to suspend judgment, to reconsider, to choose. If there is something back of the will which compels the decision one way or another, we do not have genuine freedom. One conclusion is as valid as another, and the reasoning becomes a farce. Sir Isaac Newton in the *Principia* would merely be setting down the results of mental processes over which he had no control. The reflections by which he arrived at the law of gravitation were thus not determined by choice among different equations but by some "motive" compelling the will into one direction rather than another. The only "motive" of which a reasoner like Newton is supposed to take account is that of reaching the truth, the whole truth, and nothing but the truth. Bowne's work is most distinctive in this insistence upon the necessity of freedom for thought. It means that in the process of reasoning itself the laws of reason must be followed but that these laws assume freedom. Admittedly, if one insists that all reasoning is the resultant of compelling forces without any free choice whatsoever, the farcical outcome may be the fact, and we may all be dupes in believing a freedom which does not exist; but even so the belief that we are dupes is no better founded than the belief that we are not dupes, and the debate between the two sets of dupes is farce itself. Such a disaster to thought would be a phase of anarchy worse than that which some philosophers maintain would result from freedom. Bowne used to employ the resources of his sarcasm against this argument that freedom means anarchy, even when set out with the charming and seductive rhetoric of a writer like the late John Fiske.

In 1907 Bowne took a trip around the world. Just before leaving home he told me that he had decided upon a title for his philosophy—the name "personalism." Though it may have been impudence in me to do so, I told him that the term gave no hint of the place of the objective world in his philosophy. I thought that objective idealism was still good, though personal idealism might be better. My comment got about as much consideration as it deserved, and the title "personalism" still stands. Bowne called himself a "personalist—the first of the clan in any thorough-going sense."

As the years have gone by I have felt that the change from objective idealism to personalism meant quite a swing toward Berkeley. Bowne, following Kant, conceived of space and time as forms under which the mind works, forms without existence outside of mind. Anyone who has read Berkeley knows the frequency with which he insists upon the reality of an outside world—outside finite minds, that is—and upon the impossibility of space as anything existing of itself outside of mind. In the essay upon the *Principles of Human Knowledge* and in *Siris,* the most complete statement of his idealism, Berkeley repeatedly refers to the problem of extension. In the light of this whole system it is evident enough that he has firm hold both of the externality of space for us and of the nonexistence of space in itself, but so revolutionary a doctrine as this suffers from not being treated with more emphasis than Berkeley gave it. Still, Berkeley was a pioneer in the field and could not tell in advance what parts of his system would need most elaboration. Moreover, Berkeley had a peculiarity of method which had about as many disadvantages as advantages. I refer to his admitted willingness to "humor" his readers, by which he meant starting with them by using words in the same sense as that in which the readers understood them and then by degrees slipping into them a different meaning. Sometimes this was sound pedagogical procedure, and more times not.

Both Bowne and Berkeley desired to get the emphasis off the outside world. Both taught that things must come into thought or go out of existence, and both saw the danger of making too much concession to objective orders of any stamp. "Idealism" evidently came to appear to Bowne as not a term to be held fast to. Berkeley was criticized for not making enough of the objective order even if that order had no reality outside the divine mind; for when he called the order merely one of regularity among ideas he seemed to make the regularity after all the result of an arbitrary decision by God. Indeed, Berkeley used the word "arbitrary" in this connection. The difficulty of accepting the Berkeleian idealism did not lie wholly in getting rid of a self-sufficient stuff, an unyielding matter which our common sense finds it almost impossible to give up in adjusting our notions to the idea of a regularity upheld by the divine mind. That does not seem to be enough to common sense as compared with good tough stuff which is actually "out there!" A mind, even the divine mind, might slip; solid matter never!

To anticipate somewhat, Bowne came to a quite revolutionary conception, not merely of the laws of nature, but of the laws of mind, or of the categories under which the mind works. Toward the close of his life he announced a doctrine of "transcendental empiricism" which in a decided fashion carried his philosophy to the limits. The ordinary empiricism waits upon the deliverances of experience, especially in the sense world, taking things as they come, and waiting to see what will happen next. Likewise, we have to wait upon mind, waiting to see how it reveals itself. We must not bind it by our too rigid expectations, even by the so-called categories. This does not mean doing away with the fundamental conceptions which appear to be of the native furniture of the mind, but it does mean that the categories are not iron chains which bind the mind too closely. Bowne would not have the self pressed upon by too narrow an interpretation even of its own constitution. He fought for a larger freedom —not merely that of power of choice, but an independence from rules of logic which have often made the rules first and the mind second. Here Berkeley and Bowne travel the same road, except that Bowne travels farther. It is even a question as to whether Bowne does not travel too far. For example, Bowne is sure that time is merely a form of mental activity under which we apprehend succession. Now when he is discussing such a problem as our relation to time, or when he is speaking of God's foreknowledge, he simply remarks that with God time is nothing. He does not trouble himself with the question as to whether time as we know it means anything for God. Inasmuch as time is a feature of every aspect of our existence, it does not help us much to be told that for God time does not exist. We cheerfully admit that we do not expect that because time is not real for God it shall not be real to us, but we should be gratified to think that time as inherent in our experience means something to God. If we take too lightly the question of God's relation to our time experience, we take a long step toward making him unknowable to us. It would have been more helpful if Bowne had admitted a double aspect to the divine knowing. Still, Bowne would probably have summarily dismissed this question; or he would have replied that, since we have nothing in our lives like an experience of timeless existence, all we can do is to think about it, without much content to think about except the bare assertion. If the time-form is one of the spectacles through which we look at the universe, and there is a way of looking at the universe of which we can form no conception, there is a realm of knowledge from which finite selves are shut out.

As we shuttle back and forth between those two thinkers, one seems to us now to be more stiffly logical, and then the other. We must not lose sight of the different periods in which each author wrote. Berkeley wrote his *Commonplace Book* in his early twenties. Almost everything in his philosophy appears in germ in the *Commonplace Book*. Bowne likewise as a youth wrote such a book, which contained in essence almost all that he afterward said, though this book was never published, indeed was destroyed in after years by Bowne himself. Each writer was pretty much at the outset what he afterward was seen to be. The indifference to the laws which rule the mind of God is seen in notes here and there in the *Commonplace Book*, but not in the more powerful and direct *Hylas and Philonous* written in later years. Bowne's iron quality of logic appears early in his book on Spencer. Take one sentence there to the effect that if God is infinite he can reach us and if he is finite we can reach him. This seems neat and compact; but the last half of it is likely to get us "embrangled," to use Berkeley's favorite word. Bowne's more direct arguments are about as bare as so many bullets. *Hylas and Philonous* is as strictly logical but has a richness and fullness of suggestion to which Bowne does not attain, and to which he evidently never aspired. In a passage in *Metaphysics* he declared that in philosophy one must sterilize one's intellectual instruments and proceed with antiseptic care. Bowne's keen-edged tools worked with such care. Berkeley was not always so careful, but some of the germs which

escaped his sterilization were productive and not harmful. Berkeley felt that he had started from mere sense
impressions and by strictly logical reasoning had found
out God. The logic was not always of the closest, but
the lapses were very productive.

Berkeley wrote a noble essay on *Passive Obedience*
which contains the outline of his moral conceptions as
applied to society. Obedience to constituted authority
is necessary to the welfare of mankind. The welfare
of mankind is the true social aim, and Berkeley's social
interests were as passionate as his philosophical insati-
ate stirrings. This aim is pretty well agreed upon today, but we should observe how Berkeley reaches
virtually the same conclusion as Hobbes in *Leviathan*.
Hobbes says that society has to give itself to some
central government to rule the passions of individuals
against one another. He is materialistic, with no especially theological interests whatever; his aim is to
keep human existence from being "nasty, brutish, and
short." Berkeley insists that the moral laws which
society has pretty well agreed upon for the contacts of
human beings with one another are the laws of nature
and thus the laws of God. Berkeley is arguing all
along on the basis of what may be called natural rather
than revealed religion. Statements which make such
quick identification of the laws of nature with the laws
of God fit well into an idealistic system and encourage
the hope that from these divine laws one may deduce

rules for the guidance of society. The deductions, however, cause many misgivings. Berkeley speaks of the
"higher happiness" of mankind. He seems to be
thinking of the greatest good of the greatest number;
but the content of the good is an importation into his
system of reflection which has come through the
medium of a mind steeped as Berkeley's was in the
spirit and world view of the Christian revelation.
Moreover, the laws puzzle us in their actual working
out. There is not much place for the individual taken
by himself. There are "accidental" events, admitted
by Berkeley, which complicate the process. What is
discernible is Berkeley's unquenchable interest in the
happiness of his fellow men and in Christian idealism.
The faults are those of a pioneer who sees for himself
the goals which he must keep ever before him while he
must find and beat a new path toward those goals.

Many devoted followers of Bowne feel that his
Ethics is his greatest work. The strength of Bowne
here is in his adjustment, if not his reconciliation, of
the intuitional and utilitarian schools—the intuitional
as standing for the validity of the spirit of good will
between man and man, and the utilitarian as insisting
that the methods of expressing good will must be
worked out by the utmost effort, chiefly in the study
of practical consequences. In addition, and most important of all, Bowne insists that the supreme ethical

aim is the development of normal human life to its full possibilities.

It is instructive to observe again how philosophers approach the same conclusions by different methods. The final results to be aimed at in society are the same with Bowne and Berkeley: both seek the greatest happiness of mankind, Berkeley using that very expression and Bowne speaking of the development of ι. ·rmal human life. The influence of idealism in the higher moral realm is obvious to both. The pressure of the social ideal is strong in both, though Bowne accepts this frankly and Berkeley attempts a logical method which is more faith than logic. As a single illustration, in one of the dialogues between Hylas and Philonous, Hylas asks if the acts of God toward men are not what we would call murder if they were done by men. In reply, Philonous uses the time-worn argument that, having received the boon of freedom, men may use that freedom wrongfully; then he adds that in what seems to be violence wrought by God upon a man we must remember that we cannot judge an act by itself but must ask as to the motive of the act. Then we at once make the assumption that God acts with a perfectly righteous motive. Which means that Berkeley is determined to have that kind of God. This is noble faith, but it is faith and not logic.

All through the arguments of both Bowne and Berkeley robust faith and determined reason are closely intertwined, with curious insistence now and again upon some turn of argument which seems to be almost a pet of whichever thinker is speaking. To refer again to *Hylas and Philonous,* Hylas asks if God can suffer pain, to which Philonous says "No." God sees and understands the suffering of men but cannot himself be said to suffer. Either this reply is a gratuitous contribution to the Berkeleian logic which demands impassibility in God if God is to be conceived of as perfect, or it is a simplification which does not simplify. Bowne similarly played havoc in attack upon the "fallacy of the universal." When we do away with the particulars of a class there is nothing left; but we keep assuming that there is, according to Bowne. His favorite illustration was that of the scholastic monk who believed so thoroughly in universals that he refused any fruit in particular—grapes, apples, peaches—and asked to be served with fruit in general. Upon occasion Bowne used his weapons here with devastating force, but he was likely to overwork them in handling social questions. He once replied to an attack on the modern theater by maintaining that we have to do only with theaters and the people connected with them. Do away with the people, or direct their activities into some new field, and there is no theater left. Which nobody can deny. Yet such reasoning is likely to miss the practical significance of institutional activities in society—the fact that persons are endowed with qualities which come to expression only as they act in groups; that persons acting in groups attain to degrees and qualities of achievement for good or bad that they could never reach by acting separately; that institutional activities have left records, traditions, moods in men's minds. All this means that even if we do away with the persons—the "particulars" of an institution—new conditions arise, likely to revive the institution. This is the practical aspect of a problem that the citation of the fallacy of the universal does not touch.

In commenting on the inevitability with which these idealists put more into their conclusions than their logic always warranted let us not make the fatal mistake of supposing that thinkers of an opposing school made no assumptions. We recognize that even in his strictest limitations of the activities of the self, or spirit, Berkeley placed a larger importance upon the self than *his* logic justified. I emphasize the word "his." Locke assumed a self whose activities he did not explain at all; and Hume banished the self into a mere cluster or series of impressions and then blandly continued to say, "I," "me," "myself," as if he meant just what other people meant by the words. Indeed, he could not have got his theory started or stated if he had not so used the terms. This brand of reasoning continues in abundance to this day and hour.

It has been remarked of Descartes that in his attempt to fashion a philosophy with as little help from

assumption as possible he could not get far beyond
his "I think, therefore I am." From this he could not
without assumption reach the world of things or of
persons. In thinking, we must have assumptions.
The differences between thinkers here are merely differences in degree and quality of assumptions. We
admit as we draw to a close that both Berkeley and
Bowne depend upon the assumptions of Christian believers, and that too of the evangelical type. How
could it have been otherwise? Berkeley was all his life
a servant of the church, a man completely free from
irregularities in conduct during a period when even
clerical laxity was taken as something to be expected.
The more closely we study his words and works, the
more definitely we discern the lineaments of saintliness.
Bowne was an ordained minister of an evangelical
church. Those who knew him intimately bear witness to his genuine piety, of the old-fashioned standards.
Why should it have been otherwise? If philosophers
do not, in interpreting the world and life, make Christian assumptions, they make others. One of Berkeley's
protests against the spirit of his time had to do with
what he called the "deification of matter." Whether
the assumption of spirit as back of all things does
away with materialism or not, Berkeley was quite
sure that the assumption of the supreme importance of
matter led to the lessening of spiritual interests.
Bowne's attitude was that, since philosophers must

make assumptions anyhow, it is well to make assumptions that are worth while and not to forget that we are making them.

There are minor criticisms of Berkeley which we have thought it not necessary to mention at length. Take the merriment over his belief in tar water. Notions such as his were common in his day. John Wesley was also a firm believer in the virtues of tar water. Anyone who has paid attention to the history of medical science knows that in the search for specific remedies against disease all the scientist can do is to keep looking till he finds what he is after. There is no a priori reason why quinine relieves malaria. It has been discovered that it does. We indeed see now that Berkeley was using a too deductive method in a realm where deduction is out of place. Nevertheless, *Siris,* the essay on tar water, contains some of the best phrasings of his philosophy that Berkeley left us.

The most essential difference between Bowne and Berkeley is that Berkeley worked about a half century before Kant and Bowne about a full century after Kant. The *Critique of Pure Reason* brings out into full light the activity of the self in creating objects of thought. For Berkeley ideas were purely passive. They could do nothing. They really contradicted Berkeley's protest against matter that an object which cannot do anything cannot ever report itself. Berkeley's immortal merit is that he struck the deadly blow against materialism. Moreover, he anticipated in profusion—in hints, suggestions, insights, scattered through his works —almost everything that idealism has said since his day. It is a sad loss that Bowne, with thorough understanding of Berkeley, and with the advantage of a century and a half more of philosophical discussion, was not able to finish his work on Berkeley.

WILLIAM WILBERFORCE

IN considering the evangelical movement in the eighteenth century it will not do to overlook the Clapham Sect, so named after Clapham, a country district within a short distance of London where the members of the group most often met. The word "sect" is somewhat a misnomer, inasmuch as the group was composed of merely a handful of persons without any elaborate organization.

We have been accustomed to think of the Evangelical Revival as reaching chiefly the so-called "lower" classes in England. Indeed, Wesley never took upper classes as an especially rewarding field for his effort. He was a Tory and had enjoyed high privileges, though not of a financial kind, in his home and in the schools which he had attended. His preaching, however, was more definitely aimed at the unprivileged; and those groups certainly responded most readily to his appeals. Nevertheless, the influence of the revival reached far beyond any possible contacts of Wesley himself. By the third quarter of the eighteenth century the awakening was stirring in notable, though not widespread, extent the Church of England itself. The Clapham Sect was profoundly religious, heeding the calls of the evangelical leaders to a positive religious life. The charge made against them that they were indifferent to the Established Church does not seem to be well founded. In a famous passage in *The Newcomes,* Thackeray speaks as if after their Sunday meetings before a church hour they would disperse to the chapels of the Dissenters, a statement which Canon Overton, outstanding historian of the Church of England in the eighteenth century, declares to be mistaken, insisting that the members of the sect always remained loyal to the Established Church. Again, Thackeray speaks of the entertainment in the Clapham Sect as abounding in creature comforts such as those which greeted the eyes of young Thomas Newcome when he was led to a dining room in a Clapham home, the table loaded with most costly viands. Dr. Foakes-Jackson, another historian of the Church of England, pronounces Thackeray's description substantially accurate. I quote the following from Dr. Jackson's *Anglican Church Principles*:

Clapham was a pleasant village within easy driving distance of the city of London. It was the home of wealthy merchants and bankers, who formed what is known as the Clapham Sect. The leaders were Henry Thornton (1760-1815), Member of Parliament for Southwark, Wilberforce, Lord Teignmouth, Zachary Macaulay, father of the historian, James Stephen and the Venns. Those who decry the ability of the Evangelicals would find it difficult to name a group of men whose descendants became more distinguished. The lives of the Clapham band of friends were well ordered, deeply religious, beneficent, and charitable to a degree, not entirely neglectful of material comfort. The tone of the society was serious, "not exhilarating," to quote the words of James Stephens, "except when Wilberforce was present."

In his novel of "The Newcomes," Thackeray draws an imaginary, but not inaccurate picture of the life at Clapham and a few extracts may not be out of place. Of Mrs. Newcome, he says, "To manage the great house of Hobson Bros. and Newcome; to attend to the interests of the enslaved negro; to awaken the benighted Hottentot to a sense of the truth; to convert Jews, Turks, infidels, and Papists . . . . to head all the public charities of her sect, and to do a thousand secret kindnesses that none knew of, etc." Her house was "surrounded by lawns and gardens, pineries, graperies, aviaries, luxuries of all kinds. The paradise, five miles from the Standard at Cornhill, was separated from the outer world by a thick hedge. . . . . It was a serious paradise. As you entered the gate, gravity fell on you; and decorum wrapped you in a garment of starch." No better picture could be given of the combination of lavish charity and material comfort, of energy often misdirected and good sense, of severity and real kindness of heart, of unctuous righteousness and sincere religion, which characterised the wealthy and serious world at the beginning of the nineteenth century.[1]

All that this means is that the members of the Sect belonged to the English privileged classes, and that after they had accepted the evangelical emphasis they continued to live as their class had always lived. They had been favored with more than their share of this

[1] Pp. 174-75.

world's goods, and they took the goods as naturally good and normally due them. They were fervently religious; but they lived about as their fortunate neighbors did, accepting the division of society into classes about as their ancestors—and most Englishmen for that matter—always had done.

The majority of the Church of England, however, soon began to feel that the Clapham Christians were different from themselves, and they were not pleased. At the outset it was manifest that here was a piety quite out of line with that commonly held and practiced by the membership of the Church of England. There was too much earnestness about it, too much willingness to speak of religion. While there is no indication that the Clapham group deliberately rebuked the rank and file of their fellow members of the church, their lives were a rebuke and brought the sect into disfavor. Within the general social framework of England at that day their interest in religious observances and in philanthropy got under the skin of clergy and laity alike.

I do not mean that all the upper-class piety of England was in the Clapham Sect or even had the sect for its center. Closely connected with the sect as was Granville Sharp, who did so much for the abolition of slavery, he was not himself a member—nor was Hannah More, so distinguished for her schools for the poor. By the way, Hannah More has been held on high as a noble type of saintliness by some and disparaged by others, exalted for her manifest unselfishness in service and criticized in these later days for her acceptance of the current belief as to "lower orders." It must be repeated that the sect was not thinking of social revolution but of "doing good" to men. Their intense inner experience went hand in hand with an absorbed interest in works of practical welfare.

There was not then much in the Church of England to favor any especial unselfishness of religious effort. The church was regarded as an agency for helping those in its ministry to "get on" in the world's affairs and according to the world's standards of success. There were, indeed, faithful priests; but inasmuch as their parishes were so many of them livings bestowed by patrons, they lived in subserviency to those whom they accepted as their betters.

The notion of preferment won by gaining the favor of someone rich enough to grant places runs through eighteenth-century life like a poison. Horace Walpole is supposed, in his memoirs and letters, to be a faithful chronicler of upper-class life in his century. He was constantly telling of the desires of this man or that to get this or that place, and of the intrigues and stratagems by which the place was to be secured. The Earl of Dartmouth was a sincere friend of John Wesley, and Walpole speaks more than once of the relationship between the two—a relationship, according to Walpole, which had only one conceivable bond, the desire of Wesley for position, preferably a bishopric. Still Walpole's cynicism is not to be wondered at. He but expressed the prevalent atmosphere.

Now the Clapham Sect was moved by unselfish aims. The ordinary priests of the church could not have understood the Clapham unselfishness. To some of them it was a mystery and to others a reproach. More than this, there was such distrust in the eighteenth century of what was called enthusiasm that any Christians who seemed to enjoy being Christians were looked upon with suspicion.

By being regarded as evangelicals—and they did not shrink from the name—the Clapham Sect had to suffer somewhat from the reputation of the earlier periods of the Evangelical Revival for emotional excesses. The subject of this chapter, William Wilberforce, was not born until the Wesleyan awakening as such had a history of twenty years, and it had been going more than forty years when Wilberforce joined the Clapham Sect. The excesses which had attended the preaching of the early Wesleyans had all ceased. There was no such excitement in the meetings of the sect itself. So far as concerned the relation of the sect to the outer public, the emphasis was wholly on practical tasks. The sect is not remembered in English church history today for any theological utterance or even for any outstanding pulpit oratory. It was chiefly a group of laymen who might well be called hardheaded, intent on revealing Christianity by what they got done within the limits of the actually possible.

Almost all the men who have been discussed in this series had about them traces of utopianism. As I have already said, Oglethorpe, for all his practical genius, could justly be called utopian, as could Berkeley and even Paine, whose notion of republicanism was surely utopian. I am thinking now not merely of the definite teachings of these leaders but of their qualities of temperament. Wesley in his Georgia days was far more idealistic than practical. Whitefield was probably the most practical-minded of all in this series of mine.

Now the Clapham Sect was not utopian. Its aim was to make actual changes for the good of men within the existing constitution of society. The members looked upon their duty as that of the redemption of individual souls and the improvement of human conditions. The contribution which they were to make was that of eliminating evils with the least harm to the *status quo*.

We are to consider William Wilberforce as the leader of the sect in such reform; we are to think particularly of the African slave trade, which when he began his campaign was a blight upon the moral and religious character of England and America. The study is pertinent because it shows the path which social transformations will usually have to take before the dreams of utopians can be put into material effect.

Wilberforce was born in Yorkshire in 1759, the son of a wealthy merchant. He had the privileges and advantages of financial ease and enjoyed them throughout his life. By the time he had come of age he had been graduated from Cambridge University, had won a seat in the House of Commons, had gained the friendship of William Pitt—a friendship which lasted throughout Pitt's life—and had gained fame as an orator. Slight of physique and frail in appearance, he did not arouse much anticipation as to eloquence when he rose before an audience; but he always did so much better than the audience expected that the contrast between promise and performance was all in his favor. Professor Coupland, of Cambridge, author of the best biography of Wilberforce, records that once Boswell said of Wilberforce that when he first saw him rise to make an address, he thought him a shrimp, but after the speech, he went away calling him a whale.

The earlier years of the youth of Wilberforce could be called "fast," except that there is nowhere any hint of anything that at the time would have been called immorality. There were card playing and wine drinking, which went on as matters of course in the circle in which Wilberforce had been reared, but nothing that ever was alleged against him as involving or implying scandal. The candle of the young life, however, was burning at both ends, with social activities absorbing him till far into every night. The pace was showing signs of becoming deadly.

About 1784-85 a change in Wilberforce was noticeable, at first to his intimates, and then to his acquaintances. He became thoughtful, brooding, reserved. He developed a close friendship with Isaac Milner, an evangelical, and was giving himself to long discussions with Milner about religion. There must have been some inclination in Wilberforce toward religion in his early years, for in his boyhood his mother had been afraid of the influence of evangelicals on him. However that may be, as a result of his broodings and discussions, Wilberforce experienced religious conversion, not marked by any sudden crisis, but with so complete a transformation that the former life appealed to him no longer; and with the uncompromising zeal of a new convert he seemed to be in danger of abandoning his political career for religious contemplation. William Pitt's own religious views did not find much place for contemplation but were notably sound as far as they went. Pitt never allowed anything to interfere with the friendship of himself and Wilberforce, but he could not see eye to eye with him. He wrote him during this period: "Surely the principles as well as the practice of Christianity are simple and lead not to meditation only but to action." This was good seed sown on good ground. Wilberforce found in the Clapham Sect, of which he came soon to be the leader, field for discussion of religious themes and inspiration for carrying spiritual principles into parliamentary activities. By 1786 Wilberforce, then twenty-seven years old, was back at his legislative tasks, especially interested in all problems with large humanitarian significance. He voted for Pitt's proposition for the impeachment of Warren Hastings on the ground that, as Burke so persistently argued, Hastings had not conducted his affairs in India on the basis of Britain's trusteeship for subject peoples. Just how far and how harmfully Hastings exploited the peoples of India is a subject for unending debate. Wilberforce felt sure that Hastings had not acted with a sense of obligation toward the Indian people and that the obligation was the essential in the problem.

All through the middle years of the eighteenth century the English conscience had been restive over the African slave trade, and steps had been taken to rouse that conscience to action. Lord Mansfield had decreed that no slave could set foot in England without becoming free. Granville Sharp, who took the lead in urging the sinfulness of slavery upon the moral sentiment of England, had for years been winning an increasing following. By 1787 a sort of moral gravitation seemed to press the anti-slave-trade leadership down upon Wilberforce. His religious and moral interests, his humanitarianism, his training, his genius as an orator and as a parliamentarian, were becoming obvious to the slavery haters of England. By the operation of something like inevitability he was prevailed upon to take up the war against the trade, with Parliament as the battlefield. On May 12, 1789, Wilberforce opened up the question of the slave trade before the House of Commons, and the fight was on. It is the purpose of this chapter to indicate the foes that such a fight had to meet and the questions it had to answer —all in order to show that the problems were of the same kind that always confronts the Christian statesman, and the Christian citizen, in any attempt to apply Christianity to large-scale social conditions.

To begin with, the slave trade was age-old. The oriental nations, Greece and Rome, the empires of the Middle Ages, had all accepted the trade in slaves virtually without question. At the discovery and conquest of America a new field was opened in the West Indies and the American colonies for slave labor, without which the riches of the newly discovered lands could not then be utilized. It is odd to note how feeble were the moral protests against the traffic at first. For example, look at the Spanish conquest of the southern part of the Western hemisphere, starting, let us say, in what is now Mexico. The Spanish conquerors were searching first for gold. They drove the Indians into terrible mining enterprises which involved a dreadful slavery. After the disappointment over gold the Spaniards enslaved the Indians for the sake of the cultivation of the lands, with the result that the threatened depopulation of New Spain called forth the denunciation of Las Casas in one of the most dreadful books ever written, *The Destruction of the Indies,* in which the Protector of the Indians charged that the enslavement of the Indians in West Indian islands had caused deaths by the millions. Las Casas' figures are absurd, as were most statistical estimates in the sixteenth century; but he was right about the depopulation. Now the strange feature of Las Casas' attitude is that he was willing to have Negroes captured in Africa and brought to America to lighten the lot of the Indians! In his *History of the Indies,* written many years after his own residence in New Spain, Las Casas expressed his remorse that he had ever consented to slavery for the Africans; but his case shows how hard it was for a good man—and Las Casas was a saint—to grasp the idea that it is wrong to make a slave of any man and that slavery is to be opposed wherever it is. Las Casas condemned slavery for the Indians because he had seen their sufferings with his own eyes.

Some acute turns were given the debate inside and outside of Parliament. The old argument was brought forward that slavery was an advance in historic progress, for it arose as victorious warriors kept their captives taken in battle to make slaves of them rather than to kill them. More than one debater showed the worthlessness of this argument for the purpose in hand by replying that in war the capture of prisoners is incidental, the main purpose of war being something else, whereas in the capture of African slaves the primary purpose was to capture the slaves.

Wilberforce met the general claim that slavery was a long-established custom, that it always had been and presumably always would be, by finding the facts as to the actual trade itself. He based his warfare against the slave trade on strict evidence. It is not now necessary, over a hundred years since the abolition of the traffic, to go into detailed description of the horrors of the Middle Passage, or to gaze at revolving pictures of auction blocks; but Wilberforce made all this real enough to the English mind. The pain inflicted upon Negroes was bad enough; but the degradation of Africa itself involved in enlisting native chiefs in the capture of their Negro subjects, in the sale of rum and muskets and gunpowder to Negroes in return for captives—all of this showed that the slave trade meant the denial of every responsibility of the so-called more favored peoples toward the less favored. There were those who in Wilberforce's day said that such things always had been and always would be, just as there are those today who say of war that it always has been and always has to be. The answer is that war of the present kind has never been before and does not have to be hereafter unless the wit of man is not equal to the task of so adjusting relations between nations as to make civilization and human survival under human conditions possible at all. There had not always been a slave trade of the type in Wilberforce's day. It was social insanity to think there always had to be.

It is almost incredible, this popular attitude to slavery in the eighteenth century. Look at two instances, the attitude of Lord Mansfield for one. Mansfield was the judge who had decided that no slave could set foot in England without at once becoming free. Yet Mansfield subsequently had to pass upon the case of a sea captain who had thrown overboard from his slave ship one hundred sick Negroes who would, if they had lived, have become a charge against the owners of the vessel. Mansfield ruled that the captain had acted within his legal rights. It would seem to a layman that by implication, one hundred men who would have become free the instant they might land in England could be murdered with impunity just before they landed.

The other case was that of John Newton. Newton was the captain of a slave ship who wrote in his diary about the spiritual peace he found while sailing the sea with his human cargo. Newton was converted while a slave ship captain, after a career of terrible cruelty, and became a powerful evangelical preacher. Yet Newton kept on in the slave trade for eight years after his conversion. This cannot be construed as a reflection upon Newton's sincerity. His ministry was genuinely successful, but evidently a long season was required for a change of mind to overtake his change of heart. It must not be forgotten, however, that Newton was one of Wilberforce's best counselors when the distracted young man was finding his path through the religious experience which brought out the real Wilberforce.

In the first great speech that Wilberforce made in the House of Commons on the abolition of the slave trade he received enthusiastic applause and the support of Burke, Pitt, and Fox, so that, youth as he was, he cherished bright hopes of speedy victory. Victory, however, was nearly twenty years in the future. He came to realize almost at once that "interest," to use his own expression for economic interest, blinded the eyes of his opponents, though he did not speak of them as insincere. The truth is that, while some of his opponents took the slave trade as of the natural order of man's universe because it had "always been here," others believed with equal conviction that the slave trade was one of the social constant quantities because it always paid. The "trade triangle" of Wilberforce's day was not to be abolished by brilliant oratory, even though the friends of the trade could not answer the oratory. The reader will recall that the famous "triangle" was a triple transaction: traders went to Africa carrying rum, guns, and gewgaws like brass rods and glass beads with which to buy slaves, who in turn were carried to the West Indies to pay for sugar and molasses, which coveted commodities were transported to England. Those who wanted sugar and those who got rich by the traffic painted the slave trade as a humanitarian enterprise in which the slaves themselves took delight. Wilberforce answered this by pointing to the death rate of twelve per cent of the Negroes carried in the Middle Passage.

First and last England is estimated to have carried over two million slaves from Africa to America. Now along with such immense trade goes imperialism. If the slave traffic had consisted in carrying from Africa to the West Indies slaves who had consented to go, and if it had placed them in homes where they became almost members of the household, some criticism of the trade might have been met; but the trade was speedily blighted by a deadly impersonalism, which meant that the slave was a commodity. He was a tool for work which the white man could not do. There was precious little room for that much-praised self-interest which the defenders of slavery always claimed kept the slaveowners from abusing their own property. In a large enterprise a man so deals with his human materials as to make the most out of them; personal considerations are set to one side or not taken into the account at all. There has never been a more devastating attack on the conventional arguments for the slave trade than the speeches of Wilberforce. That sea captain who appeared before Lord Mansfield to explain his drowning a hundred Negroes was acting out of strictly economic motives. The self-interest of the owners justified the murder of a hundred men.

Again, Wilberforce had to face the interlacings of slave-trade interests with scores of other interests in themselves innocent enough, and socially beneficial, but tied in with the slave trade. Slave dealers had to depend on the same material world as the most righteous of men for food and ships and equipment and financial agencies. Take away the slave traffic, the plea ran, and all these legitimate factors would suffer. Against fears like this, Wilberforce could speak so eloquently that Burke, a judge of eloquence, pronounced Wilberforce's speeches among the greatest ever delivered; John Wesley could write to Wilberforce praying God's blessing upon the antislavery war; an awakening public opinion could send a flood of petitions to Parliament in favor of abolition, yet all apparently to no avail. Parliament in 1791 voted that all the antitrade evidence should be heard again, a procedure which would require weeks and perhaps months; and though in 1792 it recognized the force of the public demand for abolition, it inserted the word "gradually" into Wilberforce's motion for abolition, thus reducing it to impotence.

What I am trying to do is to show the persistent recurrence of the forms of opposition which all attempts at the Christianization of the social order must meet.

The supporters of an antisocial cause will time and again concede the wrongness of ᴛheir cause if they can get consent to its *gradual* removal. Now is never the time. Wilberforce believed that he had won something of a victory in the "gradually" amendment by thus compelling the concession that the slave trade was wrong. This tended to stop the talk about the advantages of the slave trade to the Africans, but it also tended to stop the talk for abolition. How could a nation abolish a slave trade gradually? The rewards for smuggling were enough to make evasion cunning and persistent. Even after the abolition law was passed in 1807 policing of the seas was required till about 1860 to annihilate the trade completely. By the way, one of the side lights on the war against the trade was the unwillingness of the British pacifists to consent to sanction the use of the English war vessels against slave traders.

The crippling of his measure by the word "gradually" did not silence Wilberforce. He went forth at once on a further campaign. The vote on his motion was hardly completed when he had to meet a far more effective opposition than any he had hitherto known, one that almost nullified his efforts for a half-dozen years. In the chapter on Paine I pointed out that it was the terror aroused in England and America by the French Revolution that practically ostracized Paine. There was no danger of Wilberforce's being ostracized, but he had difficulty in getting a hearing. Burke was a determined enemy of the slave trade, but he was so thrown off his intellectual center by the French Revolution that during the later years of his career he became hysterically violent against everything French, even though the leaders of the Revolution declared for the abolition of the trade. The Revolutionary support of abolition nearly ruined Wilberforce's efforts. It does not now appear that there was serious danger of revolution in England during the French Revolution. There was, indeed, shrill outcry from the privileged classes. If Burke could be as desperately frightened as he evidently was, we can imagine the temper of the more privileged groups less intelligent than he. The masses of the English people were excited by what was going on in France, but not to the point of imitating the behavior of the French. What makes revolutions like the French is abuses like those perpetuated by the *ancien regime*. There were abuses from which the people of England suffered and against which they finally rebelled, but nothing like those which the French had borne. Discerning experts have said that England was much nearer revolution at the period of the Chartist agitation forty years after the French Revolution than at the time of the Wilberforce campaign against the slave trade.

Wilberforce had to repel the charge of French radicalism made by persons who took advantage of the

Reign of Terror to blacken any humanitarian interest that showed the least stirring of vitality. This is an old, old threat to any reform measure. We have seen it work full blast in these days since 1919. "Bolshevism" has been a term of approbrium all the more effective because those who have used it, and those who have heard it, usually have not had the slightest notion of what it has meant. After Bolshevism has come another terrifying epithet—"Communism." It may be some consolation, and it may not be, to know that terms like "Communism" and the rest have been hurled at every social progressive since historic record began.

The ferocity of the wrath of reactionary groups against men like Wilberforce is caused by fear, fear of some wild uprising which will sweep their advantages from them. Also, there is resentment against any holder of privileged position for "betraying his class" if he looks with any favor on social progress. A prominent banker in the United States, who a few years ago was sent to prison for mishandling funds not his own, expressed before his conviction the profoundest contempt for bankers who criticized his conduct—contempt because in questioning the banks they were "betraying their class." Wilberforce was charged with betraying his class.

The irony of all this is that Wilberforce was standing too loyally by his class. Officials of the Church of England complained because of his ultraorthodoxy and his ultrapiety. He was betraying the church less than were the officials who condemned him. Except in causes which had profoundly to do with human rights, Wilberforce could not be called progressive at all. In his earliest days in politics he stood with his friend Pitt against the American War of Independence. As we have seen, he supported Pitt in the impeachment of Warren Hastings; he was the head and front of the forces assailing the slave trade; he was moderately pacifist. That was all. By "moderately pacifist" I mean that he would support war only if he felt it was not for aggression. This is not a very alarming list of specifications on which to establish a charge of radicalism.

Any period when reform agitations affect money values is likely to be crazy and topsy-turvy. C. M. MacInnes, in his *England and the Slave Trade,* tells how for decades there was a bitter rivalry between Liverpool and Bristol for leadership in the slave trade, with Liverpool at last forging ahead. Whereupon the press in Bristol denounced Liverpool for bartering in human flesh. In such periods all manner of strange notions in the seething pot of public discussion jump to the surface. In a social campaign of quite recent days a radical leader was charged with teaching free love. Investigation proved that this accusation was based on a misunderstanding. A teacher who was admittedly advocating free love had the same name as the radical, whose views on sex matters were stiffly puritanical. When this confusion was brought to light the only apology the accuser made was that "it was most unfortunate that the radical had the same name as the free lover." This was tame compared to the invective poured upon those seeking for the abolition of the slave trade, as was Wilberforce, and upon those seeking for the abolition of all slavery, as were Clarkson and Sharp. Wilberforce was so moderate that he was willing, for the time being at least, to accede to the continuance of slavery where it already existed if only the ocean trade in slaves could be abolished. There is no doubt that fundamentally Wilberforce was for the outright and complete annihilation of slavery, but his program was one of gradualism until it began to appear that he could get more summary results.

A certain type of radical, even today, never gets weary of rehearsing Wilberforce's opposition to trade-unionism. We must admit that Hammond's references to Wilberforce's "horror of combinations of workers" are just, but the horror must be historically understood. To all measures looking toward the amelioration of the lot of workers in factories, for example, Wilberforce was sympathetic. He was willing to vote for any law which would help the workers, except one which would let the workers help themselves. Wilberforce's philanthropy was set in the framework of the century in which he lived. He believed that the "lower classes," in which he included the factory workers of course, had been divinely placed where they were, that it was the duty of the higher classes to help the lower, and that the duty of the lower was to accept the help gratefully and to look forward to an afterlife in which the injustices of the earthly existence would be set to rights in the glory of an eternity beyond imagination. This was the same smug preaching that the more favored have always poured out upon the less favored, and from Wilberforce's pen it makes sad reading. Inasmuch as we still hear it among Christians of more favored material position today, perhaps we had better not be too severe on Wilberforce for not living farther ahead of his class in regard to trade-unionism. Shaftesbury, who rendered larger service to industrial workers than any other Englishman of his century, detested trade unions much more intensely than did Wilberforce. Wilberforce was not an original thinker. He was a passionate humanitarian; but he had the faults as well as the excellences of the reformer who sees sharply only one object, gazes upon that object always, and makes it so much the center of all his life that other important objects appear only hazily in the outer fringes of his field of vision.

Here we note a difficulty inherent in the character of moral leaders themselves, of which they ought to take account if they can. I refer to the psychological truth that few moral leaders "have more than one fight in them." Such reformers are specialists, just as truly as leaders in other fields are specialists. I am not now referring to parliamentary leaders, who meet and deal skillfully with problem after problem as each comes up, but to the men who have acted under a compulsion toward some fundamental human need, have labored to develop public sentiment for it, have carried it along until legislators have given it final legal shape and have enacted it into law. When once this victory has been won, the leader is not likely to be further successful if he gives himself to another cause. For he does not know that other cause as he did that to which he gave the best of his life. Wilberforce, indeed, exerted vast influence after the slave trade had been abolished, but did so in the further steps toward the abolition of slavery as such, in which final steps other leaders played the leading role. Anyone who has seen outstanding fighters for the betterment of society—seen them, I mean, in the flesh and at close range—knows that they are often falling afoul of one another. Each thinks his own cause of paramount importance.

Passing to one or two further obstacles which Wilberforce had to overcome, we glance for a moment at the law's delay, or at the delay in getting the abolition sentiment enacted into law even after it had become almost irresistible. No long forward stride ahead in social progress against vested interests is likely to reach the supreme law of a land until there can be no further standing out against it. The work of Wilberforce ran through nearly twenty years. There had to be three readings of his bill both in the House of Commons and in the House of Lords, with numerous committee references. Meantime the English nation had to fight for its life against Napoleon. All conceivable delays were thrust in the road of the bill until in 1807 abolition finally prevailed because the last ounce of opposition had spent itself, worn itself out.

We all are aware that some historians will have it that in the abolition of the slave trade economic forces were the determining factors—that the trade was reaching a stage where through the exhaustion of slave-cultivated soil it would soon be no longer profitable and that the reformers got credit for a result which would have come anyhow. Nobody in these days can for an instant deny the power of economic forces in social change; but nobody can deny either that economic forces are used by men, that men act according to moral as well as economic motives, and that the leader who develops or releases the moral energies is as important as he who handles the economic instruments. Suppose the slave trade had not been abolished in 1807, and that it had been in existence when Eli Whitney invented the cotton gin. That invention made slavery more profitable than it had ever been before. After this invention attempts were made in the United States